THE WHITETAIL CHRONICLES

THE WHITETAIL CHRONICLES

Photography and Text
By
Mike Biggs

Jumpin' Buck Enterprises
Fort Worth, Texas

THE WHITETAIL CHRONICLES

Copyright © 1998 Mike Biggs

Published by:
T.P.W., Inc.
P.O.Box 330787
Fort Worth, Texas 76163-0787
Phone 1-800-433-2102

Printed in the United States of America
First Edition

Edited by Angela Casteel Biggs

Layout and design by Mike Biggs

Library of Congress Catalog Card Number: 98-90565

ISBN 0-9642915-4-1

Your heart will be thumping,
Your pulse will be jumping,
With antlers like this in your eye.
It's hard to act passive,
With headbones so massive,
And tines that reach into the sky.

He's one of a kind,
A treasure to find,
The searching has not been in vain.
Yet you'd better look twice,
He's incredibly nice,
But you'll likely not see him again.

Dedication

This book is dedicated to Angela, my wife and best friend.
Thanks for helping with the book.
And thanks for being a part of my life — the most important part.

CONTENTS

Acknowledgements

It was a big job ... and I got a lot of help from a lot of different people. How could I ever thank them enough? I could never have undertaken such a mammoth task without the help, support, tolerance, assistance and permission of all these friends. I'm truly grateful, and while it would be impossible to thank everyone who has helped along the way, I would like to extend a special thanks to a few:

Angela Casteel Biggs, George & Elizabeth Jambers, Joan & J.R. Avant, Mr. & Mrs. C.W. Cain, Bud Richter, David Morris, Jeff & Tracy Avant, Tom Mantzel, Joe & Karen Langdon, Charlie Alsheimer, John Wootters, Gene Riser, Louie Schreiner, Cricket Heumann, Billy Powell, Cliff Powell, Bill Carter, Dr. James Kroll, Dr. Harry Jacobson, Gordon Whittington, Buddy & Tommie Lowery, Jerry Smith, Lew Thompson, David Lee, Jim Hamm, Ray & Susan Murski, Tom Malouf, Dave Fulson, Mark McDonald, David & Beverly Cummings, Larry Tyler, Bill & Sharon Martindale, Larry Grimland, Allen Grimland, Marc Ellett, Bob Ellett, Thompson Temple, Kermit Klaerner, Rodney Marsh, Bruce Williams, Kelly Snodgrass, Jack Brittingham, the Doskocil family, Nelson Everett, Grady Allen, Glenn Sodd, Tom Evans, Charly McTee, Paul Hope, Gene Fuchs, Pete Wilson, Donnie Schuch, Scott & Rhonda Biggs, Wes Wynn, Don Keller, Bob Cook, Jimmy Jones, Ray Sasser, Bo & Susan Hildebrand, Betty & David Turman, Pruyn Hildebrand, Harold Jambers, Jr., Jeff Wyatt, Chuck Adams, Tim Lassetter, Dr. Charles Covert, Joe Finley, Gene Gonzalez, Mike Love, Jack Cooper, Johnny Johnson, Bill Kinney, Bob & Tracey Hild, Cheryl Davenport, Macy Ledbetter, Don & Terry Pike, Charles Schulte, John Schulte, Ward & Sue Jones, Brad Biggs, and Judy Ashworth.

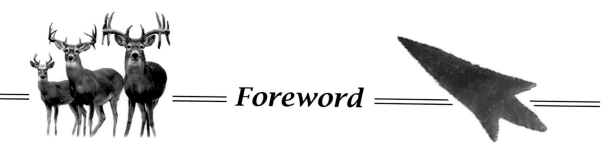

Foreword

As long as white-tailed deer are walking in the woods, there will always be humans in pursuit of them in one fashion or another. In its purest sense, it's the most natural thing in the world. We are, after all, at the top of the food chain — the top predators on the planet. And whitetails are perhaps the most appealing of all large game animals. This combination has created an ages-old cat and mouse contest between man and deer. But that's just the tip of the iceberg. The pursuit of deer has become much more than its original purpose, which was nothing more than a struggle for food, clothing and survival. In many cases the fulfillment of these needs has now become secondary to the pursuit itself. The reason is simple for those who have experienced it and difficult for those who have not, for embedded within this pursuit lies a totally different level of consciousness, separate and apart from everything else we know. And this consciousness holds wonderful secrets and surprises just waiting to be discovered.

In earlier times this pursuit was an absolute necessity. Without the evolution of early man's hunting skills, we wouldn't be here today. At first there must have been great hardships involved. Hunting tools in general were crude, and in all likelihood the reasoning abilities of very early hunters left something to be desired as well. I think we can all take pride in the fact that our most ancient ancestors worked out such viable solutions for the problems they encountered. The first crude hunting techniques marked a quantum leap from the time when they had no techniques at all. Considering what they had to work with, they came up with highly ingenious methods of hunting. Many of the tools they developed and the systems they devised are truly magnificent.

While I have no doubt that even very early humans were aesthetically attracted to white-tailed deer, their obvious first concern was their own survival. As hunters became more skillful over the ages, they must have begun to take great pride in their accomplishments. This is borne out by the wide variety of hunting rituals and celebrations that have evolved in cultures throughout the world. Man's success as a hunter has been a major issue for a very long time, and rightfully so. The development of man's hunting abilities should certainly be regarded as one of the single most important accomplishments of mankind ... ever! There have been phenomenal high-tech advancements made by man recently, but survival by hunting was a basic building block — the first brick at the base of the skyscraper. By comparison, the act of putting a man on the moon is relatively inconsequential. The development of man's hunting skills literally gave us the ability to "survive" as a species. The man on the moon, while absolutely amazing, serves primarily to satisfy our intellectual curiosity. The earlier, more basic technology provided our continued existence in order that we might have the opportunity to develop intellectual curiosities.

The essence of man-the-deer-hunter still lives on in most modern humans, though at different intensities, one to another. There are a few people who seem to have lost the hunter's instinct altogether, but not very many. While some of these few consider this loss to be a positive evolution, I view it rather as a "mutation," much like a three-legged calf or a new, unwanted strain of virus. Thankfully, the vast majority of us still retain this important ancestral heritage somewhere within our psyche, even if some people are not as aware of it as others. A fish has an innate ability to swim, but first it must be placed in water in order to utilize that ability. Likewise, the innate hunter that lives within each human must be exposed to the natural world in order to be realized. The white-tailed deer is perhaps the most ideal subject for this exposure, given his appealing nature and our very long history together. Whether you pursue deer with weapons, cameras, binoculars or simple curiosity, you will find the result to be more than satisfying. It may allow you to realize and appreciate some of your very own innate abilities well beyond your current level of understanding.

Whitetails are still highly regarded for the food and clothing which they provide, but in this day and time they are perhaps more important to us as a source of great psychological satisfaction, whether by allowing us to touch our most ancient roots through hunting or simply by offering the incredible beauty and mystique which is theirs alone. Either way, they offer food for the soul. Those of us who are lucky enough to spend time among them know that a journey through the whitetail world is a priceless gift — one of the finest that Mother Nature has to offer. Hopefully this book will help to make your journey more meaningful.

.... **Mike Biggs**

Introduction

When do you suppose the first whitetail "nut" came into being? There must have been a brief moment way back in some long forgotten time-line when an early hunter came upon a deer, and it just happened. He didn't expect it. Nobody does. Nevertheless he was struck with a flush of realization, an awakening of sorts. Here was an animal to truly stir his imagination, an animal that was so much more than mere food and clothing! Then, if he was both skillful and lucky, he probably killed it and used it for food and clothing. That was, and is, the natural order of things. But his mind-set was forever changed. He would never again view a white-tailed deer as "ordinary" or "common."

There have undoubtedly been whitetail "nuts" among us all along, ever since some early enthusiast began drawing pictures of deer on the walls of caves. In today's world there are still plenty of people who are truly inspired by deer. Many are literally "obsessed" with whitetails as only modern man could be. Whitetail images and memorabilia are pervasive throughout their homes and offices, and their "calendar year" runs from deer season to deer season.

The whitetail obsession has reached proportions never imagined by the "nuts" of yesteryear. In this "age of information," the obsession is being pursued, analyzed, savored, and fine-tuned like never before. Just as we are no longer satisfied to have only three basic flavors of ice cream, we also are no longer content to know only the basics about white-tailed deer. And just as our modern society is forging ahead in so many fields of endeavor, always pushing the envelope for more information, we of the whitetail are also forging ahead. We already know far more about deer than ever before, but we want to know more. Worse than that, like all addicts, we *have* to know more!

As a lifelong outdoorsman, and as a professional outdoor photographer and writer, I've been blessed with a very large and unique portfolio of real-life experiences with white-tailed deer. I've chased deer for over forty years, and for the last twelve years I have lived and breathed whitetails as I produced over 300,000 color photographs. I've been really fortunate to be able to observe many thousands of whitetail bucks and to actually photograph about 2,000 of them.

This whitetail-intensive lifestyle inevitably led to my first book, *"Amazing Whitetails."* The response has been phenomenal. Shortly afterward I came out with a second book, *"Whitetails In Action,"* and the momentum has continued to grow. Now I give you what may be my finest effort, *"The Whitetail Chronicles"* ... the third book in the trilogy.

This book has been twelve full years in the making. During this odyssey I've recorded some incredible moments, many of which are included here. Going further, looking deeper into the lives and lifestyles of deer, I have photographically documented the relationship between antlers and the aging process. Among other things, I have put together **actual year-to-year progressions on over 150 different individual bucks.** These studies were accomplished in a wide diversity of habitats almost entirely in the wild. The most interesting and telling of these year-to-year photographic sequences, along with their accompanying backgrounds and stories, will offer views of whitetails that have never been seen before.

Of all the nagging questions facing whitetail enthusiasts, one of the most difficult has been the true understanding of the aging process and its effects on antler development. There are countless theories and endless rumors, as well as a jumble of facts in the information marketplace. The truth, through sequential years of hard photographic evidence and detailed observation, is here in this book. I think you'll be surprised.

And there's much more! While the book is designed to be one of the most unique educational tools ever developed for whitetail management, it's also intended to be one of the most entertaining whitetail books ever published. It contains **over 500 color images** of some of the most beautiful and unusual whitetail situations you could imagine, as well as some you never even dreamed of. So go ahead. Feed your obsession. Bon Appetit!

The whitetail woods is a place of great peace, tranquility and solitude. The presence of the whitetail himself adds mystery, drama and suspense to the mix. To place yourself within it is an enigmatic experience full of calmness and serenity, yet terribly exciting.

 # WHITETAILS & QUICKSAND

Early mornings in whitetail country are often full of surprises. This photo was taken on a cold, wet morning in November. Just as the light rain and mist were beginning to let up, the sun began trying to break through the dark, dank skies. As I scanned the woods around me, this gorgeous buck appeared from nowhere as though he had materialized directly out of the mist.

Yes, fellow humans, we have been smitten by the white-tailed deer. To tell you the truth, many of us are way past smitten, beyond help of almost any kind. For some it was a gradual, almost insidious process, advancing upon us without our really knowing. For others it was more dramatic, something like a direct hit with a grand piano tossed from a second story window. In either event, we're hooked now, and this is not a catch-and-release event.

There was a time before the onset of our obsession when we didn't know much about whitetails. Then some well-meaning friend introduced us into the whitetail experience. At first it only piqued our curiosity, but with each new excursion we sank a little deeper into the whitetail quicksand. As time passed, we were gradually drawn into the irresistible and all-consuming whitetail whirlpool, like moths into an open flame. The intrigue drove us to begin spending more and more time among deer,

It's exciting as well as educational to see bucks of various ages running together like this. Relativity becomes much more apparent when bucks are visible side by side. The buck on the left is probably entering his prime at 5½ years of age. The buck in the center is older, perhaps 7½ or more. The buck at the right is a 3½-year-old with antlers that are not very impressive.

Whitetails are so agile that you never know what to expect from them. It was purely a matter of personal choice that this buck decided to crawl under the fence instead of leaping over it. He could easily leap a fence twice this high.

pursuing them in one way or another. As is commonly the case when one foe is vastly superior to the other, they easily outsmarted us. We tried again and again, and they outwitted us so easily and so frequently that the experience became more a "challenge" than just a curiosity. We tried harder, experimenting with different approaches, only to learn that whitetails are multi-talented individuals when it comes to evasion and survival tactics. We began plotting and planning ways to keep up with them. We read books, studied articles, asked questions, and most of all, we began to study the whitetails themselves at every opportunity. We found them to be much more complicated than we ever imagined.

Somewhere along this journey, our brains twitched with the reality that we were no longer *only* curious. Oh, to be sure, we *were* still curious, but it had become much more than that. The immensity of the challenge had finally dawned upon us, and further, we

There is no finer time and place to be alive and alert than early morning in whitetail country. During those magical minutes just before and after sunrise, anything can happen. This looks to be bruiser of a buck surveying the hillside. He's fully mature and muscled up, and he's probably out looking for female companionship. His neck and his ego are both tremendously swollen.

Mature bucks such as this are as different from young deer as daylight is from darkness where behavior is concerned. They are so secretive that they're rarely seen by humans.

were no longer mere observers. We had become *participants* in a complex process that's been ongoing for thousands of years. Our curiosity had evolved into a "mission" of sorts, a kind of lifestyle — a virtual *obsession*. But that's OK. If there's any such thing as a healthy obsession, surely this would be it.

In our progression as whitetail enthusiasts, we've been through many stages. In the early days, as we were basking in the glory of our discovery, we primarily just wanted to see a deer — any deer at all! We were frankly amazed that this mysterious connection to the natural world even existed. Then, as we became more experienced in the ways of deer, we wanted to see even more, especially deer with antlers. We became impatient and anxious to speed up the learning process.

Our search for knowledge moved quickly at first, and at times it almost seemed too easy.

Here is a beautiful 6x6 typical buck, probably coming into his prime at about 5½ years of age. He was caught out in the edge of an open field just before sundown on an autumn afternoon. He had followed a doe into the open, no doubt hoping to perpetuate his species. When he sensed my presence, all his energy was channeled into a mad dash back toward heavy brush and safety.

Whitetails are quite beautiful even when standing alone in stark terrain. However, put a group of them together, such as this August bachelor group, in the lush, gorgeous habitat of a rainy summer, and the beauty is overwhelming. If you're willing to brave the hot, sweltering summer days, you might be rewarded with such a sight. Bachelor groups of three to ten bucks are relatively common.

We rapidly gained access to some of the more basic concepts — their exceptional senses, the annual shedding and regrowth of antlers, the phenomenon of bucks fighting in the fall, the idea of the "rut," a general picture of their eating and resting habits, etc. Yet, as we continued with our observations, whitetails kept on surprising us as they offered up a seemingly endless array of educational tidbits.

For many of us, there was a time during our whitetail education when we prematurely began to believe that we actually knew what was going on. Such misconceptions were common, and they tended to surface when we became so totally saturated with basic knowledge that it created the illusion of wisdom. What we really had at that point was just about enough information to be dangerous. After numerous miscues and

Ah yes, sunrise and sticker points! What a way to start the day! Of course to be able to "start" a day like this, it's necessary to have been up and running for a couple of hours already.

wrong predictions, we were forced to settle down to the realization that we had only scratched the surface. There was much more yet to learn about the lives of these wonderfully complicated animals.

As we continued with our task, we encountered one mystery after another. As we observed more and more antlered bucks, many of us were puzzled by all the small-antlered bucks that we were seeing. Or perhaps I should say, we were puzzled by all of the large-antlered bucks that we were *not* seeing. At first, we didn't really understand it. Were we watching in a poor area? Was there something wrong with the local population? Were we doing something wrong? It naturally called for a little research.

When our light bulb finally illuminated, we gradually realized that most of the small-antlered bucks which we observed were simply *very young* deer. We were seeing very few mature bucks. It was quite confusing. Where *were* they? Why weren't we seeing them? Had there been some kind of die-off? Were hunters killing all the bucks with big antlers? Hardly. We finally came to understand that mature bucks were much more elusive than younger deer. And everyone has a difficult time finding them.

Those of us who were both patient and persistent eventually began to see a few larger (and older) bucks if only by accident. Over time, we've even figured out ways to find them intentionally once in a while. It's been a

Mature whitetail bucks are rarely seen within the same framework of behavioral patterns as young deer. They use different trails and travel at different times of the day. If it were not for the "rut," and the pressing biological prerogatives that force them to abandon their secrecy mode, many of these old-timers would never be seen by a human being. Thank goodness for small favors!

I spent several days in a blind near a fenceline before being rewarded with the sight of this huge mature buck. He's a high-scoring buck with a giant typical mainframe.

Dominance is an important factor all year long in the whitetail community. You can see here that the buck on the left is beginning to flinch and pull back, because the other buck is more dominant.

gradual process, but after a considerable amount of experience, it has slowly become evident that, in terms of behavior and carelessness, mature whitetail bucks are in no way similar to the young deer which we observe. Now that we have finally discovered and accepted this fact, we're ready to move on to another level of understanding. Even with the newly acquired perception that mature bucks are truly different animals, there is still much ground to cover before the new understanding really begins to take shape. Now is when the fun begins!

Everyone can experience the joy associated with the presence of white-tailed deer, whether they have much

It seems that whitetails must have a genetic predisposition for popping up in unexpected places and at unexpected times. I came upon this buck while tromping through some waist-high brush at about noon on a sunny day. I think we were both equally surprised.

Whitetails are not only mysterious animals, they also tend to inhabit mysterious environments. This beautiful typical-antlered buck was gliding silently through gnarly trees and dense, early morning fog.

knowledge or not. However, there is a point at which the level of enjoyment experienced will be proportional to the level of expertise. The more we know about deer, the more enjoyable it will be to observe and study them. It's a lot like watching a movie. We may be able to enjoy a movie to some extent by its visual effects alone, but if we understand the characters and the plot, it's always much more interesting.

As our advanced whitetail education continues, we are constantly refining and redefining the facts and interrelationships which we've discovered. By now many of the "facts" which we learned originally have *changed.*

This buck is so outrageous that he's almost beyond believability. Yet, here he stands, probably the biggest buck I've ever seen in the wild. The very possibility of seeing a buck like this, however unlikely, is what keeps us whitetail "nuts" going. He carries 28 to 30 scorable points and is very massive. I believe that his gross score is somewhere around 240.

Of course the true facts haven't really changed, but many of our perceptions about them have. The subtleties of whitetail life and behavior are so complex that it takes a thoughtful and experienced observer to accurately recognize the truths that they represent.

Of all the whitetail intrigues, antler development easily remains the most fascinating for beginners and whitetail nuts alike. We all want to know what makes antlers grow as they do. Yet, substantial pieces of this puzzle have been elusive. The details of many aspects are uncertain, and the relationships between aging and antler development are widely misunderstood.

Much of this book will be devoted to revealing the mysteries of aging and how it relates to antler development, as well as illustrating the finer points of "field-judging" whitetail bucks which are alive and in the wild. All this information is *essential* in order for us to be able to continue our whitetail education much beyond the basics. As we observe and study deer, it's impossible to truly understand what's going on unless we can factor in the age and status of the deer we're watching. Doing this will force us to see whitetails as individuals and will allow us to study them on a much more intimate basis. It will help us draw correct behavioral conclusions in the field, because many behaviors are heavily influenced by age and/or status.

As we learn the nuances of judging and aging deer, it will greatly enhance the pleasure experienced as we wade through the whitetail quicksand.

On the rare occasions when hard-antlered bucks stand in close proximity to each other, it's always much easier to determine their relative ages than if you saw them separately. The 2½-year-old buck in the foreground might seem older or larger if he was standing alone. The older buck, a 5½-year-old, might be a bit more obvious by himself, but the decision would still be less certain.

 = **WHITETAIL GENERATIONS** =

These three bucks were walking single-file down a narrow game trail on a wet, rainy day. They were lined up in ascending order ... 1½, 2½ and 3½ years of age. They were far enough apart that I couldn't get them all in focus. Even so, you can see the remarkable physical progression. Older deer frequently bring up the rear, letting younger bucks take the risk of being out front.

The natural aging process for whitetail bucks is one of the most engaging stories in the animal kingdom. It includes a little magic, lots of mystery, and plenty of surprises. The changes that occur, as bucks grow from tiny, spotted fawns to massively-antlered, muscled-up, mature animals, constitute a miraculous transformation. As we understand the changes better, our encounters with whitetails will become much more interesting.

In the past there hasn't been a lot of information available concerning the whitetail aging process — mostly a loosely held collection of generalizations that have been passed around for many years, if not generations. Part of what they contain is true, but some of the information that circulates is inaccurate. Some of the available scientific data is based on observations of captive deer, and it may or may not hold true for deer in the wild.

Whitetail bucks go through an amazing metamorphosis from the time they are born to the time of their maturity and beyond. There are a number of developmental stages, both physically and socially. Although there is a world of differences in timetables and social structuring, the stages of whitetail maturity are, to some degree, analogous to stages of development in the human maturation process.

There is much individuality among whitetail bucks. Both of these bucks are 3½ years old, but the buck on the left seems to be superior in every way. Two years later, the lesser buck had grown to a larger body weight but still had much smaller antlers.

When a buck is truly old and still healthy, his body is usually deep and thick like this one. I know from other observations that this old man is 10½ years old, but he really carries it well.

For instance, whitetail bucks which are 1½ years of age are immature by any standard, like very young children. They're curious, naive and inexperienced. Physically, they're very underdeveloped, even looking frail at times. They tend to look like does with antlers. The first set of antlers is generally inconsequential and rarely predictive, regarding future antlers.

At 2½ years of age, a whitetail buck is still very immature, much like a boy in his early teens. He's unsure about his place in the social order and fearful of older bucks. He spends a lot of effort chasing does, but he lacks finesse and experience. He rarely catches one. He's still naive but learning quickly. His skeletal bones are longer and sturdier, but his muscles aren't well developed. He has the slim, youthful look of adolescence with smooth lines and a small neck. His antlers may or may not have many points, but they're rarely substantial. In most cases they still won't tell us much about his potential.

At the age of 3½, a buck is just beginning to come into his own, perhaps like a boy in his upper teens. His bones are almost fully developed, and, depending on the individual, his muscles may have developed considerably over the last year. His body and face are just starting to look a little fuller, but overall he maintains a youthful appearance. He's trying to participate in the breeding process, but the more mature bucks will usually edge him out. A 3½-year-old is beginning to be very concerned with dominance and social rituals, particularly with his peers and any younger bucks.

The third set of antlers is of great importance to a whitetail enthusiast. This is usually the first time that a buck's antlers have a real opportunity to show substantial growth. Genetics and individuality now begin to kick in and express themselves. Generally speaking, a buck's third set of antlers will exhibit some characteristics that will be visible to one extent or another on all his future sets of antlers. Such characteristics could be related to spread, height, beam-length, a particular non-typical tendency, or any number of other nuances. Perhaps the most distinguishing feature which is now revealed is the overall shape and character of his antler "mainframe" — the way his beams and main tines come together as a unit. We can usually expect to see some variation of that mainframe configuration in all his future sets of antlers.

When a whitetail buck reaches the age of 4½, he is generally on the "edge" of maturity. At this age he is in some ways like a young man in his early to mid-20s. He's well-developed physically and in some cases is showing some bulk. His skin is tight, and he is very athletic looking. Some bucks make a quantum leap in antler development during their fourth year. In some cases the antlers may be quite large, although it would be extremely rare for the fourth set to be a buck's best possible set. Socially, a 4½-year-old is a bit "cocky" and is very much into proving his dominance at every opportunity. Of course he's not yet fully mature, and usually there are plenty of

There's a clue here. Whitetail does rarely show dominance toward bucks unless the bucks are either young, very old, or sick. This buck is neither sick nor old. He's probably just a three-year-old. The old matriarch could very well be his mother.

It's often important to factor in a buck's behavior in judging age. By his appearance alone, there was some question as to whether this buck is middle-aged or mature. However, when he intimidated two other bucks, at least one of which was obviously mature, I was able to classify him more accurately. He's a 5½-year-old buck.

older bucks to knock the wind out of his sails. In some ways this is the first year that he's really "in the game" in terms of breeding rituals and social dominance. This front-line, entry-level position, playing with the big boys, puts him at some risk. He's less experienced and generally not as strong. On top of that, he's having enough difficulty just trying to cope with his peers. As a result, mortality is relatively high for 4½-year-old bucks.

At the age of 5½, most bucks are entering true maturity, perhaps analogous to men in their early 30s. Most should be prime physical specimens. Bodies and faces are now filled out substantially. The fullness extends from their briskets to their haunches, and most will have large, swollen necks during the rut. Many have developed quite an "attitude." They are in the middle of things socially and are attempting to optimize their status at all times. Dominance behavior is rampant. Genetic propensity and maturity are really starting to show in their antlers. Some may have non-typical characteristics for the very first time. Bucks that didn't make a large gain in last year's antlers probably will this year. Some will make a big leap during both years. By this time, bucks have become very cautious and secretive.

By the age of 6½, most bucks have entered full-blown maturity, like men in their upper 30s or early 40s. In some ways they're the same as they were at 5½, except that they just have more of *everything*. Some bucks may produce their lifetime-best set of antlers this year, but for others that experience is yet to come. Their faces are beginning to show some character. The skin may be getting a little loose, and jowls may be beginning to show. At this age many bucks are dripping with "attitude" and seem to consider themselves more or less invincible until proven otherwise. Any other buck shouldn't mess with them unless they're ready to fight. The survival skills of 6½-year-old bucks are finely tuned. They're secretive beyond words,

The buck above has antlers which are so surrealistically large that his body may look smaller than it really is. He's a 6½-year-old buck whose body weight is probably average for late season. The early-season 5½-year-old buck to the right shows more normal proportioning between his body and his antlers.

frequently becoming nocturnal. If it weren't for the rut, we'd probably never see most of them.

At age 7½ and beyond, whitetail bucks are like old men, 50 and over. Surprisingly, many of these "old" bucks continue to flourish for several years, producing even larger antlers as they go, in many cases. There was a time not too long ago when the popular press allowed that whitetail bucks reached their prime and then promptly wasted away. However, I haven't necessarily found this to be the case. In many respects, "old" bucks are the most interesting age class of all. They tend to have a lot of character and personality. You can see the maturity in their faces, and their bodies

Sometimes a single aspect can show us a lot. The huge neck on this buck tells us that he is mature. He is 6½ years old, and those wraparound beams are about 27 inches long.

range from full-blown to gigantic. Also, oddly enough, many bucks develop antler characteristics in their older years that they never exhibited at a younger age. Old bucks commonly develop non-typical antler characteristics, such as sticker points and drop tines, *for the very first time* at age 7½, 8½ or 9½. As long as their physical health is good, antlers tend to be massive and gnarly. It's very common for the size of an old buck's antlers to vary a little up and down between the ages of 7½ and 12½, depending on nutritional factors and individual health. Never count an old buck out just because he lost some antler size in a given year. He may come back larger than ever.

The social standing of old bucks depends largely on their health and their individual personalities. Some bucks are still dominant and in the breeding pool until age 10½ or 12½. The ones that remain dominant become *extremely* overbearing. They show more "attitude" than you could carry in a bucket.

Antler size is not necessarily commensurate with age. Considering his stature, facial characteristics, and behavior, I believe that the beautiful 10-pointer on the left is a 4½-year-old. The other buck has lesser antlers but is likely to be 5½ years old or more.

At first glance this buck looks too thin to be 5½ years old, but that's his correct age based on several previous years of observation. There are a number of factors to consider. First, it's summertime. His neck is small and his hair is short. Also, he's really stretched out, and that makes him look tighter and younger. And he just happens to be a small-bodied individual.

Others are so intimidated and physically bullied by healthier, prime bucks that they become very reclusive, almost invisible.

Old bucks frequently exhibit limps and scars from battles fought. They're often arthritic and move around stiffly. Still, if you're like me, it's almost impossible to look at a really old buck without getting a smile on your face, just imagining the times that he's been through.

There are many factors to consider in determining and studying the various age classes of whitetail bucks. You can learn far more about a buck from his body, facial characteristics, and behavior than you ever will by looking at his antlers. And don't forget to figure in the effects of seasonal influences and whitetail individuality. These elements should always be considered in judging whitetail bucks of any age. Also, like humans, deer don't all mature at exactly the same rate. There are early bloomers and late bloomers, and there are exceptions to every rule. Please bear in mind that whatever I offer regarding one age class or another is based on examples which are the most "usual and customary" expectations, but there will always be exceptions.

For most purposes, whitetail bucks should be placed into four basic classifications with regard to age:

"Young" .... (1½ and 2½ **years**)
"Middle-aged" .... (3½ and 4½ **years**)
"Mature" .... (5½ and 6½ **years**)
"Old" .... (7½ **years and older**)

These are logical groupings and serve as simple points of reference for communicating age. There are many occasions when bucks within these groups are difficult to differentiate anyway. When viewed from this perspective, the whitetail aging process will start to come into focus.

1 ½ *YEARS OLD*

This is a very normal "long-yearling," or 1 ½-year-old whitetail buck. At this stage he looks pretty skinny. Always take special care in judging a running or leaping buck. When muscles are tensed for such athletics, young bucks tend to look a little older, and older bucks tend to look a little younger.

This is a particularly nice 1 ½-year-old buck with 10 symmetrical points and slightly long brow tines. His body conformation is also attractive. It's usually not a good idea to try to predict future antler development based on the first set of antlers, but this buck's prognosis is likely to be good where antlers are concerned.

Yearling bucks tend to look "frail" compared to older deer, and this look is somewhat exaggerated in the summertime. Some of the later-born fawns carry that "baby deer" look through their first fall as an antlered buck. Their stature is not unlike that of an average doe, except for the antlers. It's fairly common for first-timers, such as the buck on the right, to have some type of antler deformity.

2½ YEARS OLD

The running buck just above is a typical example of a normal 2½-year-old buck. He's still skinny and doesn't have much of a neck, but overall he has just a little more muscle than a yearling. His antlers are only slightly less than average for this age. The buck on the left is slightly above average in the antler department. His beams are a little longer than usual, and he has a double brow tine as well as a small extra burr point. These things don't amount to much, but it's not particularly common to see "extra" points of any kind on a whitetail buck until he is 3½ years old or more. This buck also has a very attractive body conformation and prominent facial markings. He'll be easy to recognize in the future.

Both of these 2½-year-old bucks are definitely better than average, especially the one above. With a big body and a very substantial rack carrying 12 points, he is almost certainly destined to be a "super buck." He's so far off the charts that he will probably be a monster at age 3½. By comparison the buck on the left seems small, but he's actually fairly massive and well above average for his age. His left antler is slightly abnormal.

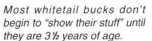

Most whitetail bucks don't begin to "show their stuff" until they are 3½ years of age.

When whitetail bucks reach the age of 3½, they are beginning to show some muscle mass for the first time. Even so, they are still quite slender and taut compared to mature deer. The buck at the upper left has extremely good antlers for his age with 15 points and good mass. He's a good example of how seasonal influences can affect a buck's appearance. He could easily be mistaken for a 2½-year-old without the knowledge that this photo was taken in late winter when he would naturally be quite thin. Though he has only eight points, the buck at the upper right is also outstanding. Unfortunately, he was harvested by a hunter who mistakenly believed him to be an older deer because of his antler size. The buck at the lower right has broken off a drop tine from his left side.

4½ YEARS OLD

At age 4½ bucks are showing a considerable amount of muscle tone, and their skeletal bones have just about reached full size. They're still smooth and sleek in appearance. The antlers now begin to show their genetic propensities, and some can be quite large even though the bucks are not yet truly mature. All four bucks on this page have exceptional antlers. Scorewise, the buck at the top left is about 145 gross, top right is in the 165-170 range, lower left is roughly 150-155, and lower right is 155-160.

By the time whitetail bucks have reached 5½ years of age, their bodies are filled out, and they are strong and muscular. These are typical examples with some minor variations. The buck at the upper right exhibits a smaller neck only because the photo was taken very early in the season. The buck at the lower right is full-blown bodywise, but he exhibits genetically inferior antlers.

6½ YEARS OLD

At age 6½ most bucks are filled-out, muscular and stout. In many cases, antlers are at or near their prime. Most whitetails of this age group have become very secretive, even nocturnal. The buck at the upper left is a prime example, a very nice 5x6 typical. The buck at the upper right has a particularly well-developed, muscular body, but his antlers are not very impressive by comparison. The buck at the bottom of the page has such a full, deep body that it makes his legs look short. He was observed for many years and was always a slick, smooth, substantial eight-pointer until the age of 11½ when he added double drop tines.

When bucks become seriously old, it's easy to differentiate them from younger deer. Body weights can be extremely heavy but not always. The buck at the upper left is thought to be 9½ years old based on previous sightings. Notice his jowls, sway back and pot belly. He perpetually holds his ears in a flopped-down position. Flopped ears are frequently seen on very old deer. The buck at the upper right could fool you. It's late season and he is alert, tense and stretched out, looking smooth and younger than he is. He's at least 7½. The 7½-year-old buck at the bottom left has lost a lot of weight during the rut. Oddly enough, the buck at the bottom right is the same deer as in the bottom left photo, but at 8½ he has recovered his weight and increased the size of his antlers.

7½ + YEARS OLD

When whitetail bucks are lucky enough to reach the ripe old age of 7½ or more, they frequently become so secretive that they're rarely seen. Many of them become nocturnal. The ones that are still participating in the breeding process may be intercepted occasionally because of the careless behavior associated with the rut. However, some are no longer active participants, particularly if younger, stronger, 5½- and 6½-year-old bucks have "whipped" them out of the process. Those beat-up, older bucks get so reclusive that it can be almost impossible to find them until you finally find their bones in later years.

Truly old whitetails usually have a very distinctive look to them with a lot of character showing, both physically and in their behavior. They frequently have sagging jowls and loose skin around their faces. They're pot-bellied and sway-backed, and they often carry scars from previous wounds. It's very common for them to be limping or walking stiffly as though they have arthritis, because they probably do.

The buck on the right is an extremely old character. His exact age is not known, but it's clear that he's quite an old-timer. I would estimate that he is at least 9½ or 10½ years of age, maybe more. He still looks very healthy. You have to wonder what he might have looked like in his prime.

When really old bucks remain healthy, their bodies can reach enormous proportions. The large-bodied buck just above is a good example. He's so heavy that even as he stretches out severely in this panicked, mad dash, he cannot look smooth and thin. Look at the ridge of hair standing straight up on his back. His age is unknown, but he's at least 7½, probably more.

Here is a slightly different perspective on the aging of whitetail bucks — "Aging by Silhouette." When looking at deer in this manner, there are fewer distractions to deal with. Everything is reduced down to body shape, body size, antlers and in some cases, facial shapes. The buck at the upper left is obviously an older deer, even though his antlers are poor. The upper right buck, with his deep body, is at least mature, maybe older. The middle photo easily differentiates the mature buck from the two much younger bucks. The bottom picture shows a mature buck at the left, a 3½-year-old in the center, and a prime 6½-year-old to the right.

The top photo on this page shows a unique circumstance. I know from other observations that the "old" buck on the right is an incredible 11½ years old. He's a full 10 years older than the yearling buck on the left. The middle picture shows a "mature" buck and an "old" buck. The mature buck on the left is 5½, and I know the old buck on the right to be 9½. The 5½-year-old buck has better antlers, but notice the belly and jowls of the buck on the right. The buck at the bottom left is 5½ years old, but it's very late in the season and he's run down from the rut. He has no belly. The lower right buck is a healthy 5½-year-old as seen during the pre-rut period.

Always keep a close watch on whitetail behavior for it offers many clues to a buck's age class and/or status. The one-eyed buck at the top left is an ancient warrior. At 10½ he's got a "bad" attitude, and he's really letting it show as he cocks his ears, his head and his tail and forcefully strides directly toward another buck. He probably hasn't taken any "guff" from another buck in years. The 7½-year-old buck at the upper right and the 9½-year-old buck at the lower left are showing the same type of attitude. In the photo at the bottom right, the buck on the right is making a submissive gesture toward the older, more dominant deer on the left. The submissive buck has better antlers, but this behavior helps to confirm that he is only middle-aged.

Behavior alone cannot tell you the exact age of a buck, but it can help you classify a buck generally as young, middle-aged, mature, or old. Perhaps more importantly, the very presence of social behavior signifies that there are two or more animals present, and observation will easily tell you their relative ages. Their reactions to each other will give you the pecking order, and to a large degree, it will parallel the age order. Both bucks at the top, as well as the buck at the bottom right, are all 5½-year-olds. You can see that they're all acting very aggressively. It seems that dominance behavior tends to become substantially more aggressive at this age. The bottom left photo shows an old buck threatening a middle-aged, but better-antlered, buck.

In judging the ages of whitetail bucks, it's very important to take seasonal factors into account. The same buck will have a considerably different appearance in the summer, in early fall, during the pre-rut period, during the rut, just after the rut, and later in the winter. The weight fluctuations and changes in muscle tone can be very dramatic. The photo of the mature buck at the top left was taken during the peak of the rut. The top-right photo of the same buck was taken just three weeks later, but take a look at the weight loss and the change in muscle tone. The bucks at the bottom are fully mature, but both have lost a great deal of weight during a rough winter.

A considerable change in appearance takes place between early fall and time for the rut. The 4½-year-old buck at the top of the page was seen in mid-September (left) and again about six weeks later (right). He lost some belly but gained substantial fullness in his neck and face. His muscle tone is entirely different. The 6½-year-old buck at the bottom of the page shows a similar circumstance. He changed a lot from mid-September (left) to early November (right). He looks like a different animal in November.

June 12

July 10

June 26

August 15

September 12

Here it is! — the miracle of antler growth as illustrated by a nice, typical, five-year-old buck. The top left photo shows him in early June. The top center photo was taken in late June, and the top right shows an early July shot. Antlers are growing ninety-to-nothing during this period. The fast-growing antler tips are shiny and bulbous. In the bottom left photo his antlers are completely grown and in the process of hardening and drying out. The bottom right photograph shows his brand-new hard antlers.

ANTLERS, AGING & GENETICS

August 10

September 10

June 24

The annual antler regeneration process is a complex and amazing spectacle. This handsome 10-pointer makes it look simple. Take a close look and notice how he changes. His antlers may be the center of attention, but there are also other changes taking place. His coloration, overall muscle tone and stature are considerably different in September than they were in June.

Antlers are the fastest growing bones in the world. Yep, *THE* fastest! You can almost see them grow. In fact, there are times when you can actually notice a measurable difference after only one or two days. If you can locate a buck in early summer and manage to see him every week or so through September, you'll be totally impressed. There's a powerful sense of wonder that comes with the process. You'll be telling your friends all about it.

It seems as though we can hardly speak of antlers without using superlatives such as biggest, tallest, widest, or heaviest. Whenever we think of whitetail antlers in any kind of an abstract sense, we are invariably imagining them on a *grand* scale of one type or another. It's only natural. These grand versions of whitetail antlers, whether real or imagined, are the fuel that keeps our fires blazing.

Whitetails have plenty of intriguing qualities, but 99 times out of 100, the bottom line for whitetail "nuts" is *ANTLERS*. A given set is as unique as any rare collectible, and the "world-class" versions will take your breath away. The

Is this the beginning or the end? When bucks shed their antlers at the end of the season, the antlers don't always fall at the same time. It's common to see one-antlered bucks during this period. There's only a short period of time when bucks have absolutely no antlers at all. After shedding the old antlers, the pedicels quickly heal over, and the renewal process promptly gets under way.

It doesn't take long before the new set of antlers becomes visible from a distance. Even at this stage in early June, it is apparent that this big-bodied buck is a mature animal.

truly outrageous examples of antler development are rare, but they do occur. Their appearance in one place or another is, to a large extent, unpredictable. We gripe and complain when we can't find them, but it's this very same unpredictability that creates the challenge and the romance that we savor. We're usually smiling as we complain.

In order to find extremely large antlers, we generally need to find older bucks. And the older the bucks, the more exponentially difficult the job becomes. The pursuit of mature whitetail bucks is altogether exciting, challenging, frustrating, humbling and rewarding. As difficult tasks go, this one is pretty much in a league of its own.

Our journey down this path should begin with education. The more we understand about the aging process and how it impacts the lives of older bucks, the more competent we will become in our pursuit of them. An understanding of the nuances of antler

As the summer progresses, so do the rapidly growing velvet antlers. They grow from the tips, and it's always evident where the antlers are growing the fastest because they are bulbous and shiny at those spots. This buck appears destined to become an impressive animal in the fall. It's only early July and he's already showing a substantial 6x7 typical mainframe.

development and structure will help in field-judging bucks that we encounter. A comprehension of the relationship between antler development and the natural aging process will enhance our field-judging ability even more, and it will give us a broader perspective on whitetails as a whole.

As whitetail enthusiasts and managers, we have to realize that, where whitetail studies are concerned, there are exceptions to virtually every rule that has ever been spoken, written, or discovered in a research program. This doesn't make the rules invalid. It simply means that there is an "art" to understanding the science.

Whitetail managers are making every effort to enlarge their populations of mature bucks. It is an elemental fact in developing a deer herd with a larger upper-age class that young and

In late summer the antlers stop growing and begin the hardening process. The blood supply shuts off at the pedicels, and the velvet dries out. When he's ready, each buck vigorously removes his velvet.

Here are two different views of a very interesting non-typical buck with forks, long kickers and a drop tine. I saw him in August and again in September. He's a mature 6½-year-old and scores better than you might imagine. As is so frequently the case with non-typicals, some points are not fully visible. He was taken by a hunter later in the year and carried a gross score near 180.

middle-aged bucks must be protected from harvest efforts. The ONLY way that this "protection" can be carried out is through the ability of ranchers, managers, guides and hunters to recognize age classes accurately and to exercise proper restraint.

With minor variations, generally accepted whitetail management principles ("GAWMP") have been written up repeatedly throughout the popular press. We've all been hammered quite diligently with the age, nutrition and genetics equation, as well as information on population management, habitat management, supplemental feeding and other management practices. This is all good information, and we need to know it. However, the whitetail public at large has begun to grasp much of the basic GAWMP concept quite well. It may be time for some new perspective and perhaps even some

additional level of understanding, not to displace GAWMP but to add to it.

Of the three primary management components, nutrition may be the best understood. The cause and effect relationships are easy to see, and nutrition can be easily manipulated.

Everyone is curious about the genetic component. It's a complex issue, and current understanding is lacking in many respects. In some cases different research studies have even produced conflicting information. Among other things, scientists are working on isolating the genes responsible for antler growth and structure. At this point, there aren't many practical methods of exercising control over genetics. Selective harvest helps, but it's a slow process. Transplantation, artificial insemination and other techniques are being utilized, but they can be expensive, and there are no guarantees.

Here's an example of a nice four-year-old buck in two stages of antler development — August and September. Early on, he originally began growing a double beam on his right side, but it was so tight against the primary beam that they eventually grew together before the velvet antlers reached maturity.

The "age" component of whitetail management is simple to understand, and it's the easiest by far to control. Generally speaking, older bucks have bigger antlers. So don't kill them when they're young. Then, they'll probably get older. But how do you know an older buck from a younger one? Not much attention has been given to the art and science of "field-aging" whitetail bucks which are alive and in the wild.

Very little information has been published showing the true relationship between the aging of whitetail bucks and the commensurate antler development throughout the various stages of their lives. Yet, this is essential information. Without it, GAWMP practitioners cannot even begin to optimize their efforts.

In understanding the makeup of a herd, it's important to recognize the particular antler styles and nuances that exist in the area. As you observe and study different bucks over time, you'll begin to see genetic influences and tendencies. You'll recognize some bucks as direct descendants of others that you've seen, but you'll also notice a constantly changing array of new styles and configurations from the same gene pool. Once in a great while, something like you've **never** seen before will walk out of the woods. And *that's* what it's all about!

Sometimes a buck will bump an antler pedicel very early in the antler growing cycle. If it's damaged, but not profoundly, the result may be a double beam. Double beams are relatively scarce and are rarely repeated the following season. These photos show the same buck at age 3½ on the left and 4½ on the right. Did you recognize him at age 4½ with a larger rack and a double beam?

Many things can and do happen to whitetail antlers during the velvet growth period. As agile and graceful as they are, there are times, if only rarely, when deer stumble, fall or bump into something. When velvet antlers suffer serious injuries, the outcome is unpredictable, and in some cases it can be permanent. The photo on the left shows a substantial double-beamed buck.

The photos on this page represent an interesting case study on the passing of antler genetics. Both left-hand photographs show the same buck. The upper left shows him as a "middle-aged" buck (4½) and the lower left shows him when he was older (7½). He was observed occasionally on a hunted ranch and was placed on the "protected" list as far as hunting was concerned. He was easily recognizable with flat, laid-out beams and a wide spread. He usually had 10 typical points and one to three forked tines. The photos on the right show an entirely different buck. They were taken from the same blind but several years later, after the left-hand buck had met his demise. The upper right photo shows the new buck at "middle-age" (4½), and the lower right shows him at maturity (5½). As you can see, he made a remarkable one-year gain. He has the same flat, laid-out beams and wide spread as the earlier buck. During each of the three years that he's been observed, he has had two or three forked tines. His facial characteristics and body conformation are similar to those of the other buck. He even shows a similar, very dominant attitude, as well as a propensity to break some of his antler points each year, just as the earlier buck did. So, are they directly related, or did they just come out of the same gene pool? In back-dating the new buck's age to determine his birth year, it shows that he was born just a few months after the earlier buck died. No other bucks with these characteristics have been seen in the area.

Each of the photos on this page shows bucks which appear to be closely related, if not from the same mold. The two mature bucks at the top exhibit similar antler height and mainframe shape as well as similar body conformation. The middle photo shows a large 5½-year-old, non-typical buck on the right with numerous sticker points and long beams. His 3½-year-old cohort is also very large for his age and also carries multiple sticker points and long beams. The bottom picture shows an old buck on the right and a middle-aged buck to the left. They both carry 10 typical points and good brow tines, and each has a sticker point on his right side. Sightings of bucks which are similar are not rare, but in the majority of situations, we would expect to see a wide variety of very different looking antlers, even within the same gene pool.

There is an enormous amount of interest in whitetail genetics and how it may affect future antler development within a given deer herd. Many times in nature the connection is unquestionably evident. The top photo is yet another example of bucks which share many common physical traits, including antler characteristics. We wouldn't really expect to see identical bucks within a herd, rather, bucks which share many variations of similar traits. We also see another quite different phenomenon occurring. The photo at the bottom shows three different middle-aged bucks, all living within the same gene pool, which are about as different as they could be. There is a super wide 11-pointer with short tines, a medium wide 8-pointer with average tine length, and a tall-tined 12-pointer with sticker points and a narrow spread.

As a species, whitetails have a very large range of genetic diversity. Even with so many combinations possible, some dominant traits are passed on intact from one generation to the next, but the majority of physical characteristics which are acquired through heredity are new, hybrid traits created from new combinations of genes.

The question of the day is this ... How do desired, or aesthetically pleasing, characteristics, such as the drop tines on these two bucks, get passed along? Or do they? If so, then how can we hasten the process through whitetail management?

So far, research has not given us a clear answer. In my own long-term observations, I've noticed some possible clues, but they are far from definitive. Even though whitetails are capable of reproduction at a very young age, the re-appearance of genetic traits seems to take place over a relatively long cycle — perhaps something in the range of six to nine years. Major antler traits are frequently not apparent until age 4½ or older. Even then, the buck with the traits may not successfully pass them along until he is fully mature. Finally, in the event that these traits are successfully passed, they may not be apparent until the offspring is 4½ years old or more.

The large drop-tine buck at the top of the left-hand page was observed as a dominant buck for several years. The photo shows him at age 6½, and this was the first time he had grown a drop tine. At 7½ he grew double drop tines. During those two years I wasn't aware of any other drop-tine bucks in the area. This buck died the following winter. Over the next four years, only one drop-tine buck was seen in the area, but five years after the death of the old man, at least five different bucks with drop tines were observed there. IF he was the sire to this line of drop-tine bucks, it seems apparent that he didn't pass this characteristic along until he was quite old. And the offspring didn't exhibit their drop tines until they were several years old. If this concept were to hold true, then the younger, 4½-year-old buck at the bottom left may not have passed along anything yet. Unless he has the opportunity to live a few more years, he might never do so.

Both of the dominant 5½-year-old bucks on this page tell a different story. Each buck had distinctive antler characteristics which were not common in his area, and both of them lived for one more season. Yet, some four years after their demise, there still have been no sightings of any new bucks with similar traits.

Non-typical bucks are always difficult to field-judge. This buck, like so many others, is likely to fool you. He's mature. At least that much is clear. But there are several substantial points which are lined up with others and therefore hidden from view. That's one of the main problems in judging big non-typicals. You can rarely see all the points. Even when you can, the points which curve or aim toward you are difficult to figure. He was taken by a hunter later in the season, and his gross score was measured at over 200 inches.

BONES OF CONTENTION

This is such a pretty buck — a classic, long-beamed, 5x5 typical with wide spread antlers. He's not an extremely high scoring buck, but he's not bad either, at about 150 gross. I was lucky to see him on a perfect, frosty November morning. This was the only close-up shot I was able to get. He followed a doe out of the timber and past my blind, stopping momentarily before chasing her into the distance.

Given the broad range of different shapes and sizes that whitetail antlers come in, it was inevitable that we would devise systems to measure and compare them. The old basic whitetail descriptions, such as *"whopper"* or *"monster,"* aren't nearly enough anymore. Depending on personal preferences, the implication might be that "he was wide," or "he was heavy," or "he had lots of points." Such subjective terms could mean one thing to the person describing the deer and something completely different to the person listening. As a result, we have refined the process to make it more comprehensible. Now the question is ... "How big *is* big?" Today's basic description is likely to be much more informative, something like: "He was a 150-class 10-pointer with a 20-inch spread and a couple of sticker points."

Over the years there have been a number of different efforts to systematize the way we

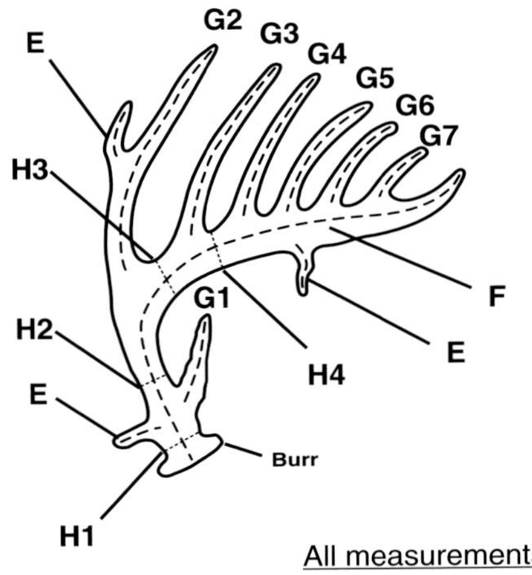

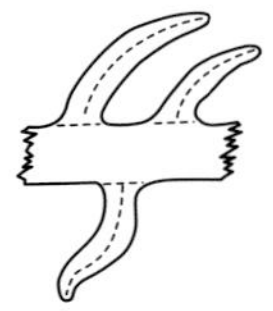

measurement of points

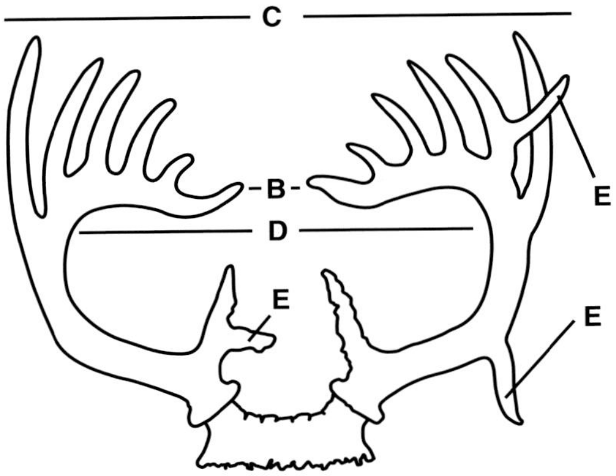

All measurements are made in one-eighth-inch increments.

	Left Antler	Right Antler
Length of first abnormal point	4	1
Length of second abnormal point	9⁶/₈	1
Length of third abnormal point		3²/₈
Length of fourth abnormal point ..		
Length of fifth abnormal point		
Length of sixth abnormal point ...		
Length of seventh abnormal point		
		19

	Left Antler	Right Antler
*A. Number of points	7 x	8
B. Tip to tip spread		7⁶/₈
C. Widest outside spread		17⁴/₈
D. Inside spread of main beams..........		15⁶/₈
†X. Inside spread credit..........................		15⁶/₈
E. Total lengths of all abnormal points		

	Left Antler	Right Antler	Difference
F. Length of main beams	23	23⁴/₈	⁴/₈
G-1. Length of first point	6²/₈	5	1²/₈
G-2. Length of second point	11²/₈	10²/₈	1
G-3. Length of third point	10²/₈	10⁶/₈	⁴/₈
G-4. Length of fourth point	4⁴/₈	6⁶/₈	2²/₈
G-5. Length of fifth point			
G-6. Length of sixth point			
G-7. Length of seventh point			
✔H-1. Smallest circumference between burr and first point	5²/₈	5	²/₈
✔H-2. Smallest circumference between first and second point	4⁴/₈	4⁴/₈	
✔H-3. Smallest circumference between second and third point	4¹/₈	4³/₈	²/₈
✔H-4. Smallest circumference between third and fourth point	3⁶/₈	4	²/₈
Totals	72⁷/₈	74¹/₈	
TD. Total of all differences for F's, G's and H's			6²/₈

Gross Typical Score = (X + both F's + all G's + all H's) 162⁶/₈

Gross Non-typical Score = (Gross Typical Score, + E) 181⁶/₈

Net Typical Score = (Gross Typical Score, minus E, minus TD) 137⁴/₈

Net Non-typical Score = (Gross Typical Score, + E, minus TD) 175⁴/₈

Points must be at least one inch long in order to be counted. †Inside spread credit may not exceed the length of the longest beam. ✔Exactly four circumferences per side are used, no more, no less. If brow tine is missing, measure both H-1 and H-2 at the smallest place between burr and G-2. If G-4 is missing, take H-4 measurement halfway between G-3 and tip of main beam.

To score a buck, you can put together a tally sheet something like the one on this page, or you can simply use a piece of blank paper and draw columns on it, once the process is understood. Verify the methods of computation for yourself by comparing the numbers in this actual example. These measurements were taken from the non-typical buck pictured at the bottom of page 60 after he was taken by a hunter. As illustrated here, gross non-typical score is the single most accurate indicator of true antler size.

All three of the deer on this page are very nice examples of classic "typical" bucks. The two 5x5 bucks at the top have approximately the same gross score, somewhere in the 165-170 range. The right-hand buck has more tine length, but the left-hand buck has more mass. The buck at the bottom right, even though he's a 6x6, scores a little less, closer to 160.

measure, compare and communicate about whitetail antlers. Most of them never gained broad, mainstream acceptance and eventually disappeared. The primary measuring and scoring system that is generally accepted today is the Boone & Crockett system, usually referred to as simply "B&C." The Boone & Crockett Club maintains records on all North American big game animals, including white-tailed deer. The system has its share of critics, but overall the club is well respected, and the system is widely used.

The Pope & Young Club, "P&Y," which maintains similar records exclusively for bowhunters, is also well known. For measuring and scoring, the P&Y system has

adopted the same methodology as that used by B&C. The only difference is that the minimum entry criteria is lower for the bowhunting record books.

The scoring systems currently in use are based on measurements of the inside spread of the beams, the lengths of the beams, four circumferences from each beam, and the lengths of all points. All measurements are recorded to the nearest one-eighth of an inch, and a point must be a minimum of one inch long to be included. Under the B&C system, symmetry is highly regarded, and this particular facet has become a source of considerable debate among whitetail nuts.

The buck on the left has only two abnormal points, but they are so prominent that he seems quite "non-typical." The buck below has five abnormal points: the two "hooks" on his G-2s, the very long extra point coming off the base of his left G-2, and two burr points. His actual gross score, as calculated on page 58, is 181⁶/₈.

For purposes of scoring and comparing, antlers are classified into either "typical" or "non-typical" categories. B&C maintains a listing in their record book for each category, and individual entries are ranked in order of score. To be listed in "The Book" requires a minimum "net" score of 170 for typicals and 195 for non-typicals. P&Y also maintains listings, and its minimum entry scores are 125 and 150, respectively.

Typical antlers are defined as having a "normal" configuration ... two beams with an in-line series of more or less vertical tines emanating from the tops of the beams. Any growth or variation beyond this normal configuration is considered to

The left antler from the giant non-typical buck on the right was found after the season, and it added up to a gross score of 109 by itself. His total gross score may be around 240. The huge-bodied buck below has long, curling brow tines, a drop tine and long points that go down the back of his head. He's bigger than he looks. His official gross score is 211.

Super tall tines are real attention getters, especially when they rest atop beams that are also relatively high. This August buck has a giant eight-point frame with a very small G-4 on the left and one small sticker point on his left G-2. He will probably gross a little over 150.

be non-typical. This would include all extra points such as stickers, drop tines, extra beams or burr points.

As we go through the mechanics of developing scores, you may find it helpful to refer to the sample scoring sheet on page 58. To begin, all typical measurements plus the inside spread credit are combined to get the **"gross typical"** score. As typical measurements are made on each side, the corresponding numbers are compared, and the "differences" are totaled up. If the rack has any non-typical points, their measurements are added together to get an "abnormal points" total. Then, in order to figure the **"net typical"** score, both the "differences" total and the "abnormal points" total are *subtracted* from the "gross typical" score.

In the event that antlers are being scored as non-typical, start again with the "gross typical" score. The "differences" total is still *subtracted*, but the "abnormal points" total is now *added* to derive the final **"net non-typical"** score. The choice of whether to score a buck as a non-typical or a typical is optional.

If all this seems confusing to you, you're not alone. Not only do these scoring methods show a preference for symmetry, they actually *penalize* a buck for a lack of it. These symmetry considerations were arbitrary on the part of the original B&C system founders, and they apparently found pure symmetry to be more aesthetically pleasing than actual antler size. Because of these constraints, there are many great bucks that don't make "The Book" which are actually larger than other bucks that do.

There is a way to remain happy within the system even if you don't

The buck just above has phenomenally long tines which are "bladed" or palmated. The buck at the bottom right is very wide but has extremely short tines. It seems to be a very common trade-off for wide antlers to have short tines and for narrower antlers to have taller tines.

agree with all the symmetry constraints — Just ignore them and make no deductions. Add the "abnormal points" total to the "gross typical" score and the result will be the **"gross non-typical"** score. This number is the most accurate indicator of true, overall antler size. While gross scores have no official status where the record books are concerned,

I've noticed that within the whitetail fraternity at large, more and more people are referring to antlers in terms of "gross" score alone. And in almost all cases they're talking about "gross non-typical" score. It seems that the majority of whitetail nuts are of the opinion that a buck should get credit for any and all antler that he grows, symmetrical or not. Further, just about everyone I know actually *prefers* antlers with extra points and character.

Even with the net versus gross controversy, the measuring methodology of the B&C system still gives us the most straightforward technique for developing scores. Also, the B&C record books are filled with

When a buck is extremely massive, the circumference element of scoring becomes obvious and important. The deer on the left is likely the most massive-antlered buck I've ever seen in the wild. He's a monster! A sight like this will definitely make your day. His eight circumferences may total as much as 50 inches! A more common total might be around 28 or 29 inches. The thin-antlered buck on the right leans toward the other extreme. Even though he is mature, his total mass measurements are only about 23 to 24 inches.

Beam length can be a little hard to grasp in the field with all the various shapes and turns. The buck at the upper left has well-developed points but very short beams. The long-beamed buck just above is fairly obvious, as is the one at the bottom left.

useful, fascinating information. They give us benchmarks to study and compare, and show us the upper limits, at least up to this point. Some people may not agree completely with the system, but the majority of whitetail nuts are reasonably content. Most are more interested in the deer themselves than in any personal ranking in "The Book."

This is not to say that no one is interested in net scores and whether or not a buck makes "The Book." That's not the case at all. Many people *are* interested. Even so, common sense and practicality have come to dictate that most communications and references regarding antlers be based on gross score alone, especially in the field.

Gross score is a highly valuable tool when used as a "shorthand" method of describing

While in the field looking for big deer, nothing can grab you by the throat like a set of super wide antlers. A really wide rack always seems impressive, whether it has anything else or not. The buck at the top is a super wide ten-pointer, maybe 25 inches, but with short tines his gross score is only in the low 140s. The eight-pointer at the lower left has a medium spread, about 18 inches. He's a 130-class buck. The lower right buck is extremely narrow, but with double beams and 14 points, he grosses somewhere in the 150s.

If you only got a quick glance at this buck from the angle in the left photo, you wouldn't be getting your money's worth. It gives the offhand appearance of a small-framed 10-pointer, maybe 11. However, when he turns to the side, he reveals a full-blown, quite symmetrical set of 7x7 typical antlers with beams that shoot forward. Even with short tines, his gross score is in the high 150s.

a buck. It's the best way to convey a true mental picture. Gross score tells you the actual size. A couple more descriptive facts, perhaps the number of points and the spread, and you've got a quick, concise idea of the magnitude of a buck's antlers. When having the same conversation using net score references, the information must constantly be qualified or appended in order to know the true scope of the antlers.

In terms of judging whitetails in the field, you can estimate gross much more quickly and easily than net. If you have plenty of time to evaluate a buck, you may be able to refine your judgement a little, but usually, plenty of time is not an option.

In determining "How big is big?" in the field, a hunter must bring together a unique blend of skills, several of which are quite complex by themselves. Basically, each new attempt at field-judging brings to bear the culmination of all previous whitetail experi-

ences. Inconveniences such as poor visibility and physical discomfort are frequently a problem, and time pressure usually weighs heavily. The job requires focus and concentration ... no small matter, considering the mental and emotional demons that are constantly conspiring to thwart the process.

Accurately judging bucks in the field is an art, a science and the ability to combine the two disciplines logically and quickly. It entails the judging of aesthetic qualities as well as the determination of antler measurements based on estimated points of reference. This ability evolves through experience. Study and practice in any way that you can, but nothing nurtures success more than actual in-the-field experience.

The concept of field-judging bucks is usually perceived primarily as field-judging "antlers," but the evolution of the process has come to mean that we are also "field-aging" the buck. Without this component, the whole idea would be of very little value where whitetail management is concerned. It's not enough to know only the antler score. That would be a short-sighted approach, useful only to one who wants to find a buck with big antlers and get him on the ground regardless of management objectives. Knowing the approximate age class of a buck can help you confirm or deny your judgment of his antlers. Also, the more total information you have about each buck, the more you'll understand about the health, status and trends of the entire herd.

No single element can give you the exact age of a wild buck, and the same is true when field-judging antler size or score. Both efforts require a combination of assessments which are interrelated. Characteristics first have to be sized up individually, then collectively.

There are a variety of different "yard-sticks" which are used in field-judging antlers. Antler dimensions are often compared to body parts which are relatively consistent in size from one buck to another, such as ear length, nose length, spread between the ear tips, eye diameter, and so on. It works quite well, but the physical characteristics of whitetails vary so substantially that reliability will only be commensurate with the experience of the practitioner. For instance, I have personally measured the distance from ear tip to ear tip on many bucks and have found a range from about 14 inches all the way up to 19 inches — and this was done in Texas alone! I'm sure the range is equally wide on the larger-bodied northern bucks. Of course, with today's management, 250 pound bucks aren't nearly as rare in Texas as they once were.

Here is another buck that could fool you badly in a field-judging situation. And yes, I'm positive it's the same buck. The photo on the left was taken late, right at dusk, as he went over a hill. His antlers were silhouetted, and he seemed quite large. However, I saw him the next day from a blind and what a surprise! He's a very small-bodied buck with thin antlers and moderate measurements. The moody light and the angle of the antlers had been very deceiving. At best, he is a 130-class buck.

This mature buck is quite interesting, even though he is a "cull" or "management" buck by almost any definition. He has no brow tines whatsoever, and his points are uneven, but look at those beams — heavy, wide and long. There are very few six-pointers with this much size and character. I saw him only once or twice a year for four years, and his antlers were always about the same.

Look at the huge, blocky body on this buck! His antler frame is also large, but he's only a giant six-pointer. For management purposes, most programs would have him removed.

knowledge of behavior and aging to good advantage in refining field decisions.

Accurate field-judging ability is the primary mechanism which makes it possible to differentiate individual bucks and to selectively control the harvest in order to achieve desired management objectives. Without this ability, we could neither understand the current condition of a herd nor follow its trends.

Field-judging lets us identify the so-called "cull" or "management" bucks — those bucks which are not considered to have acceptable genetic potential for the future good of the herd. The definition of a "management" buck is based on several considerations, and it varies from one management plan to another. It's based partially on whitetail biology and accurate knowledge of the current dynamics of the herd. Personal preferences are also considered. A set of minimum standards is designated, and bucks which fall below those standards are targeted for harvest. Antler characteristics of 1 ½ and 2 ½-year-old bucks are not usually very indicative of actual potential, so these age classes are usually totally protected. Middle-aged bucks with desired antler characteristics are also protected in hopes that they will mature, become dominant and spread their genes. Personal choices are made as to what types of bucks will be removed and what types will be protected.

I mentioned earlier the widely used practice of using gross score as a verbal/mental shorthand in describing and considering antlers. We can take this verbal/mental shorthand a step further to increase our efficiency even more. It's really nothing new.

Many of us have been using the terminology for a long time. Like many others, I have a tendency to group bucks into "score classes." It's a very convenient habit. Furthermore, who would we be trying to kid by thinking we could field-judge wild deer so accurately as to be precise, anyway? Some people are pretty good, but it's not an exact science. Even with experienced judges, the tendency is to "nail" some scores, be fairly close most of the time, and once in a while to miss by a country mile. We make every effort to learn from our mistakes, but there are too many variables to ever achieve perfection. It makes sense to generalize just a bit, since we're estimating anyway.

The most common field-scoring vernacular, using "score classes," is to speak of gross scores in multiples of tens ... for instance, 130-class, 140-class, 150-class, etc. There are

The buck on the left is an extremely symmetrical 10-pointer with almost no deductions. The buck on the right is a considerably larger-framed 12-pointer, but he's not particularly symmetrical. If you heard their "net" scores without having seen them, it would sound as though they were about the same size, both netting in the high 130s. On the other hand, if you heard their "gross" scores, which are in the high 130s on the left and in the low 150s on the right, you'd be getting a much more accurate picture.

These are difficult situations when trying to judge antler score. The buck on the left is running away, up and over a hilltop, chin up, head high and ears back. At a glance, he looks quite large. However, closer examination reveals that he grosses only in the mid to upper 140s. He's very asymmetrical, and his net score is only in the 120s. The buck on the right is walking away in thick fog with his head high and his ears back. This one lives up to his first impression, gross-scoring in the low to mid-160s with very few deductions.

no exact rules here, but when we speak of a 150-class buck most people are usually considering his gross score as being about 150 or better, perhaps somewhere within the 150s. If it's very close, say 148 or 149, it would usually be included. Some people take it as a "plus or minus five points" proposition. Either way, it gets you into the ballpark quickly. A few people get carried away with themselves and begin reporting *exact* scores. Overall, when in the field, the "tens" categories are more practical.

At first it's necessary to wrestle with all the small details of judging antlers and ages, over and over, in order to get started. However, the processes eventually will become more automatic. Given that you rarely have the time to do all the detailed comparisons and computations anyway, you'll soon begin to see bucks directly in terms of age classes and score

classes. It may seem a little unlikely at first, but with practice (and frequent verification) you'll be able to recognize these classes almost instantly. Keep working at it, and there will be a time when you can see a buck and intuitively know that he is a "middle-aged, 140-class 10-pointer with an 18-inch spread." You'll hardly even have to think about it.

The photo layouts over the next ten pages will help you get the visual "feel" of the different score classes. There is a page of examples for each score class from 110 to 200. The score class is noted at the top of each page. First, study the individual details in each group. You'll see that many different antler styles can produce similar scores. Then, try comparing them as groups, and you'll begin to notice the incremental changes in overall size as you glance from group to group.

Bucks in the 110-class group are usually, but not always, younger deer. They range from large-framed six-pointers to short-tined ten-pointers. Did you happen to notice that one of the bucks on this page is much older than the others? It's the buck at the bottom left. At 6½ years of age, he is stout and dominant, but he has a very small antler frame, probably as a result of genetics.

120 CLASS

The gross scores of bucks which are three years old or more tend to average in the 120s. Sometimes one exceptional characteristic, such as long brow tines or long G-2s, will put a buck into this category. Other times, short points or a lack of points will keep a buck from ever reaching beyond this level. Occasionally a wide, 120-class buck with short points can appear to be much larger.

A 130-class buck is above average. Many middle-aged bucks fall into this category, but it's populated by older bucks as well. Even an exceptional 2½-year-old makes it into this class occasionally. It's interesting to see how differently the various antlers on this page are put together, yet, when the measurements are added up, they all end up within just a few inches of each other.

140 CLASS

A great many of the bucks which reach maturity under good nutritional conditions "top-out" in the 140s. At first glance a 140-class eight-pointer, such as the buck at the upper right, appears larger than a 140-class ten-pointer, because what he lacks in points is made up with a larger overall frame. This concept holds true for all classes, but the difference is more noticeable in the larger sizes.

Most whitetail "nuts" tend to classify bucks which are 150 or better as truly outstanding. In terms of overall percentages, not many bucks get past the 150 mark. Look at the enormous body size of the early-fall buck at the bottom left. The "fewer points, larger frame" concept is certainly at work here. His eight-point mainframe is larger than any of the multi-pointed bucks around him.

160 CLASS

The buck just above was seriously injured in a fight.

At each increasing class level, the number of bucks in existence decreases greatly. Whatever small percentage of bucks have the potential to gross 150, only a small percentage of those have the potential to make it to 160, and so on. When bucks reach the 160-class category, they are usually beginning to show some exaggerated features, such as extreme tine length or beam length.

When bucks reach the 170-class level, their antler configurations are likely to be almost anything. The buck at the upper left makes it with heavy mass, 13 points and long, sweeping beams. The buck at the upper right does it with 17 substantial points. The lower-left buck does it with long beams and tine length, and the buck at the lower right makes the mark with about 20 inches of drop tines.

180-190 CLASS

We're into the "super buck" category now. Bucks of this size and larger are freaks of nature and as such are very rare. All the bucks on this page are solidly into the 180-190 class. I had the opportunity to measure the sheds from the buck at the bottom left . The final tally was 188 gross. I also measured the antlers on the skull of the buck at the bottom right, and the total was 191 gross.

This is the stratosphere of whitetail fantasy. These bucks are beyond "super." The buck at the upper left has very short points, but there are over twenty of them. His massive beams are roughly 29 inches. His shed antlers were measured at 207 gross. The buck at the upper right has terrific beams, tine length and mass. His sheds were measured at 202 gross. The bottom buck was found dead of natural causes. He had over 20 measurable points, and his gross score was 198. He was only 3½ years old.

MONSTER CLASS

Once in a great while a buck turns up that practically defies description. He's a "monster." What else could you call him? Only one of these three bucks has actually been measured, and he's the one at the upper right. With 17 massive points and super long beams, his gross score was 221. The buck at the upper left is estimated at 220-230 gross, and the bottom buck is estimated at 240 gross.

As is so often the case, this buck wasn't especially impressive as a 2½-year-old. There was very little indication of antler potential. At 3½ he began to show his character — thick, rough bases, short brow tines, a basket-rack mainframe with short to average beams, and a hint of future sticker points. At 4½ he was a slightly larger version of the previous year, still with 10 typical points. At 5½ he made substantial gains, growing a full, heavy, 5x5 typical frame with three sticker points. He was a 150-class buck at age 5½.

REAL DEER & THE TIMES
OF THEIR LIVES

4½

5½

6½

This buck always carried himself in a stately fashion. It was one of his hallmarks. His rack was very recognizable from age 4½ to 6½. At 4½ he was just showing a glimpse of the short G-4s to come. The sticker on his right G-2 was always present, but the sticker on his left G-2 came only at 5½, as did the split brow tine. With short beams and short G-4s, his gross score at 6½ was in the low to mid-130s.

Whitetails and their lifestyles have surprised and entertained us all. As we move through the different phases of whitetail education, we can only be amazed at each new level. The beauty is astonishing, the behaviors are intriguing, and we remain wide-eyed in wonder at the entire antler regeneration process. Now it's time to cover some new territory. We're going to take a look at the actual development that individual whitetails go through as they age from year to year. All aspects of their lives are affected by, and change with, the aging process. If we understand the process more clearly, it will give us great insight into the facets of their lives.

I've been studying the whitetail aging process, along with antler development and behavior, for many years. I've photographed and studied deer at numerous locations, and some of the same places were revisited year after year. Every effort was made to find bucks which had been seen before and to document their progress. Fortunately, several of the places where this work was done had management plans that allowed many bucks to reach upper age classes. It's been my privilege to watch a large number of wild bucks mature over time spans varying from two or three years to as many as nine or ten years. It's been an entrancing, educational experience. This chapter includes 65 of the most interesting year-to-year aging sequences

that I've been able to put together over the years. I believe you'll find this information to be quite revealing — unlike anything you've ever seen before. You'll be able to study wild bucks as they age and mature right before your eyes. Take a really close look, and you may begin to see whitetails a little differently.

Just to be sure that readers can follow my presentation easily and confidently, let me lay out a few basic premises. The "field-aging" of whitetail bucks is not an exact science. In fact, it may be more art than science, considering the large amount of whitetail individuality that exists. Think about it in human terms for just a moment. Pick out any age group and try to formulate a set of rules that will define *all* humans of that age group. It's impossible. There's too much individuality. It's the same with deer. Yet, as we've discussed, there are many clues which can be used to estimate or determine a buck's probable age. With experience these estimates can be very accurate.

If you like lots of vertical points, then you're going to love this buck. Even at age 2½, he was a remarkable little buck with seven typical points on each side. Unfortunately, no photo is available for that year. At 3½ he had a 6x6 typical frame with forks on the right G-2 and G-3 and another fork on the left G-3. At 4½ he had a slightly larger, similar version, except that the left fork had moved from the G-3 to the G-2. At 5½ he became larger with an 8x9 mainframe. The left side changed again, growing nine essentially vertical points. Medium tine lengths, heavy mass and 17 points put his gross score somewhere around 170.

What a face! Check out those eyes! I saw this buck for only two years before he disappeared. Still, a look at those two years illustrates an interesting point. At age 4½ his antlers were lopsided with five typical points plus a sticker on his right side and four typical points on his left side. His left G-3 was long and out of proportion. There is a tendency to look at antlers which are uneven like these and imagine that they will always be uneven. Sometimes that will be true. However, in many cases the antlers will even out with age. This buck was more symmetrical at age 5½, growing a nice 5x5 typical rack that grosses in the low to mid-150s.

Naturally, I have some advantages that readers would not be aware of simply by studying the photo layouts. I've watched many of these deer at great length, and their interactive behavior has been factored into my decision making process. By seeing them in action and watching their reactions to various challenges, I know their individual attitudes and body language by heart. Even so, the photographs alone offer a tremendous amount of information, and great care has been taken in selecting photos with angles and perspectives that will make these studies and comparisons clear and meaningful.

These estimates of ages are not guaranteed to be precise in all cases. For anyone to imply that they could perform such a task flawlessly would be a bit presumptuous. There are too many variables. However, I'm confident that the vast majority of these estimates are correct,

and that the few which may be imprecise are in no case off by more than one year. The general tendency is to be conservative if not exact.

During all the years that I collected this data, there was a constant search for every possible source of verification to either confirm or deny estimates of both age and antler size for the bucks in this study. Any time one of them was taken by a hunter or found dead of natural causes, the facts were gathered. When someone found a shed antler from one of these bucks, measurements were taken. At every opportunity, notes were compared with wildlife biologists, ranchers, game managers and others who had experience and expertise in judging whitetails.

Comparing the social behavior and physical appearance of individual bucks from year to year can help confirm their age and status. Several years of looking at the same buck will

At age 4½ this otherwise handsome buck severely damaged his left antler. There must have been a traumatic injury to the antler while in velvet. A severe injury like this can sometimes ruin a set of antlers for life. I didn't see him at 5½, but at age 6½ he looked terrific. He was a solid 150-class buck with a 5x6 typical frame and big, bladed brow tines. He was dominant and highly visible that season. The next year I saw him only one time. His antler size had decreased a little, and his body weight had diminished considerably compared to the previous year. There were probably several contributing factors. It was a drought year, and less nutrition was available. Also, he had run himself down the previous fall while participating in the rut so vigorously. The effects of that type of stress can carry over to the next year. And of course he was getting older. Late one afternoon near the end of the season, a hunter saw what appeared to be a large, mature, spike-antlered buck, and he shot it. When the buck was retrieved, this was the buck he had killed. Incredibly, this buck had broken off BOTH beams exactly flush with his huge brow tines.

When I first saw this buck I felt there was a possibility that he might grow outstanding antlers at maturity. After all, how many 3½-year-olds have a wide, fully developed, 5x5 typical mainframe with double drop tines outside the spread of their ears. Very few 3½-year-old bucks exhibit drop tines in any form. I went back to the ranch the following year with high hopes. However, I never laid an eye on him. As far as I know, no one on the ranch ever saw this buck during the entire season. We assumed that he had died of natural causes. The following year I went back, and guess what? Here came the double-drop-tine buck, prancing out of the woods in exactly the same place where I had seen him two years before. He was a handsome 5½-year-old buck, but he didn't develop as well as I had hoped. He added a little spread and beam length but didn't achieve any gigantic proportions. His gross score was in the mid to high 140s.

tell you far more about him than any single year ever could. However, *finding* the same wild buck for several years is not an easy task.

Some of the aging sequences in this chapter are contained within a single page. Others are presented on double-page spreads. All presentations are made in a manner that allows you to read the narrative and compare all available years at one time with no turning of pages. The small yellow circle on each photo indicates the estimated age of the buck at that time.

A few sequences are missing one or more years. In some cases I saw the deer but was unable to get a photograph. In other cases I couldn't find the deer at all. Whitetails are wily

by nature, and bucks disappear for many reasons. The bucks in these sequences are wild deer living mostly in hunted populations. There have been many times when a buck has disappeared for an entire season, only to magically re-appear the next year. Many other old friends have disappeared forever. I've learned to accept each new sighting as a gift, pure and simple.

The year-to-year aging sequences shown on the following pages tell some very interesting, true stories. There's a broad cross-section of whitetail types included, and they come from many different areas. None of the bucks in the sequences shown in this chapter live in research programs or pens. **All of these are "real" deer.**

As a 2½-year-old, this buck had a nice eight-point frame. Then, at 3½, he was a solid ten-pointer. At 4½ he was considerably better, and it seemed that he would just keep on growing. However, at 5½ he stayed about the same. It was a drought year, and even though the ranch was supplementally fed, a lack of nutritional diversity may have affected him. He wasn't seen again.

This buck had loads of character, both in his antlers and in his attitude. He was a "fighter!" The very first time I ever saw him, at age 4½, he had broken a main beam. He seemed to have been a straight 5x5 typical that year. The next season, at 5½, he had a 5x5 typical frame plus a sticker on the right G-2 and a fork on the left G-2. He was seriously hurt in a fight and had a huge bloody sore on his neck for weeks. At 6½ he was considerably more massive, a 5x6 typical with a big drop tine. Even then, the tip of his left G-4 was broken from fighting. He was "ruling the roost" in his area. At the age of 7½, he changed again. There were two drop tines, common-base points, and stickers — 16 scorable points altogether. Soon after I took the photo at the bottom right, he disappeared and wasn't seen again. About a year later, his skull was found locked with that of another buck. His gross score was 191.

3½

4½

5½

To have been a fairly ordinary eight-pointer at age 3½, this buck made a pretty good jump at age 4½ when he went to a solid 5x5 typical mainframe with a small drop tine. As a 5½-year-old, he had a 5x6 typical frame with a drop tine and extra brow points on his left side. There was also an extra two-inch point behind his right brow tine. With 15 points, average mass and slightly long beams, his gross score was probably in the upper 140s. Where he'll go from here is anybody's guess, but there's a chance that his non-typical characteristics may increase. The way his beams reach forward, he could have a 6x6 typical frame before he's finished. This buck has very attractive facial markings and is easy to identify. He also has exhibited an interesting personality. At 3½ and 4½, he was very curious and pushy, even for a middle-aged buck. He spent a lot of time in sparring matches with virtually every other buck which came into sight, large or small. At 5½ he gained a tremendous amount of body size and became fairly dominant. Though I searched for him on numerous occasions, I saw him only one time, in early November, when I took the photo on the right. Then he just disappeared. Neither I nor the game manager saw this buck for over two months, thinking that perhaps he had been killed by either a hunter or another buck. Then, as though by magic, he walked out of the brush in late January, looking beat up and run down from the rut but otherwise healthy. It's amazing how bucks can disappear so completely and then re-appear as though they had never left. He probably got side-tracked during rutting activities and just didn't make it back until the rut was over.

At age 3½ this buck was a fairly small nine-pointer, a typical 4x5. The next year, at 4½, he made a quantum leap in antler size. His right side, which had been the smaller side the year before, jumped to six points, while the left side remained at five. The last three points on the right were clustered together. At age 5½ he improved again. He still had a 5x6 typical rack, but the numbers had switched sides. The right beam seemed a little shorter at 5½. Overall he was beautiful. His gross score was likely in the low to mid-150s. This buck was usually a solitary animal, but when he did encounter other bucks, he was very dominant. From the time he was 5½ he was **extremely** intolerant of any other bucks. I saw him "hooking" other bucks in the rump on several occasions as he chased them out of sight. Most bucks were deathly afraid of him. At 6½ his antlers became weird on the right side with the G-2 forking, then forking again. There was no G-3. Nevertheless, he was still the meanest buck in the valley. I never saw him again after that December.

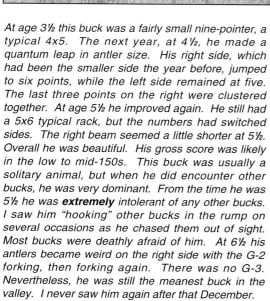

3½

5½

4½

It's funny how highly recognizable bucks, such as this one, can live in a heavily watched area, yet rarely be seen. Then, as though someone flipped a magic switch, they suddenly become visible. That's what happened with this buck. I rarely saw him until he was 5½. He was a small 4x4 typical at age 3½. He improved at 4½ to become a 4x5 with two major sticker points. At 5½ he was even larger, but the left sticker moved from the G-2 to the G-3. From the first time I saw him, he seemed to have a very nonchalant attitude and was never very dominant. Though still showing some promise, he was taken by a hunter at age 5½, because he had been gored by another buck, and it was feared that he would not survive the injury. I wonder if his beams might have eventually touched, or even crossed, had he lived longer. Beams that turn in substantially are usually longer than they appear. At 5½ his gross score was in the mid-140s.

I observed this buck in an area of mature hardwoods interspersed with open fields and meadows. At age 3½ I saw him only one time, in velvet, as a 4x4 typical. At 4½ he was a 4x5 and was showing a tendency for long tines. I never saw him at age 5½. Then, at 6½, he re-appeared with a substantial 5x5 typical frame plus one abnormal point. His gross score at 6½ was in the 140s. At age 7½ he reverted back to a 4x4 mainframe with long G-2s and a gross score in the 130s. Then he disappeared forever.

95

This buck is easy to recognize. It's strange how many times you quickly recognize a buck without really knowing what it was about him that you remembered. Some of the key elements on this buck are his black-tipped ears, a slightly pointed nose, very little white around his eyes and nose, and a small but bright throat patch. At age 4½ he has 11 points and grosses in the low 130s.

I watched this buck for four years in a row in an area known for producing primarily small deer. At age 2½ he must have damaged his antlers while in velvet, breaking and malforming some points. He came back strongly at 3½ with a 5x5 typical frame plus horizontal sticker points on both beams. At 4½ he added small kickers on both G-2s, but the horizontal sticker disappeared from his left beam. At 5½ he's lost one kicker but has horizontal stickers on both beams again. He's an outstanding 150-class typical buck.

I guess we can just throw away the rule book on this one. This buck has maintained a youthful appearance throughout his entire life. He looked much the same at age 6½ as he did at age 3½. The two "running" photos, which were taken three years apart, look almost the same, yet I'm certain that it's the same buck. I also saw him at 5½ but couldn't get a picture. He looked about the same then. At 7½ he still has the slim lines of a much younger deer. This is the kind of buck that can really fool a manager who doesn't know his deer well. If not recognized, this type of deer might be protected as a "middle-aged" buck, year after year, as he continually breeds his mediocre genetics back into the herd. His gross score is usually in the 120 to 130 range.

This is a strange little buck. And I say "little," not because of his antlers, but because of his petite physical stature. Even as a 3½-year-old he was not much bigger than a large fawn. He looked a lot like a doe, but I could see that he wasn't. He expressed a tendency for high beams and burr points early on, and by 5½ he had fairly substantial antlers, especially considering his small body size. At age 5½ he was a low-end, 140-class buck. I saw him only once at 6½, in velvet, and never saw him again.

3½

4½

5½

If there is any such thing as a "sissy" among whitetail bucks, then this buck would probably qualify. He kept very much to himself, and when other bucks did come close, he acted very fearful and subordinate. I doubt that he did any breeding at all. He was easy to recognize with the bright white rings around his eyes and the extra amount of bright white on his nose. He was probably even more recognizable by his tentative posture and timid attitude. At the age of 3½ he was an average-looking buck, a 4x5 typical with one small sticker point on his left G-3. At 4½ his rack became lopsided with a fork on the right G-3 and stubby brow tines that looked as though they were trying to split. At 5½ he put on so much body weight that it made him look like he had short legs. His antlers were still very uneven, but now they were configured differently. The 4x5 typical portion of his frame had switched sides, and now there was a horizontal sticker point on the right G-2. His gross score was in the high 120s.

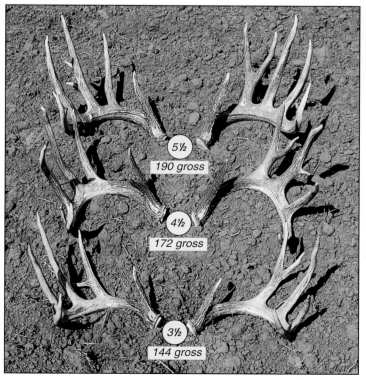

This is an outstanding buck. Too bad he's been so difficult to find and observe. I've seen very little of him, but not because I wasn't trying. When he was 4½ years old I saw him only one time from a blind, just at dark. That's when I took the top left photo. He was seen and described by ranch hands when he was 5½, and I spent a lot of time waiting patiently in the areas where he had been seen. But all I got was a 10-second glimpse at flat dark one evening. I was impressed, and it made me sit at that location for days, but I didn't see him again that year. They've been very lucky at the ranch about finding this buck's sheds. A ranch hand found his sheds from age 5½ just as he began to run over them with a tractor. Another year came, and again I spent much time and effort trying to find this giant buck. It seemed that I never would, but he finally showed up at a waterhole where I was sitting. I saw him on three different afternoons. He was slightly more non-typical at 6½ with 18 scorable points. His gross score was in the low 190s.

I observed this buck for eight seasons. Some years I barely saw him, and other years I saw him many times. One year I didn't see him at all. He was quite a character, easily recognized physically and equally recognizable by his behavior and attitude. He had beautiful colors and markings, with black-edged ears and a brilliant white throat patch. He always held his head high as though he were confident and proud. He was a muscular buck with an attitude and was a dominant "fighter" from the time he was 4½ years of age.

He had 9, 10 or 11 typical points each year with no non-typical tendencies. It's unusual for extremely old bucks to have no abnormal points at all. His antler size varied up and down from the age of 5½ to 10½, usually grossing in the 140s. He was injured several times over the years, and when he was 8½ he lost his right eye in one of his many battles. He survived quite well and remained dominant for the next 2½ years. His antler size actually increased at age 10½. He died of natural causes the following summer.

With short, upright beams and eight slick points at 3½ and 4½, this buck had the look that we see with many of the bucks which become lifetime eight-pointers. Yet, at age 5½, for some unknown reason, a small drop tine appeared. Maybe it was just a one-year anomaly due to some minor injury. On the other hand, it might be a harbinger of things to come. We'll just have to wait and see. He's a large-bodied deer, and the sight of the long G-2s on those high beams makes him look larger than he really is, which is about 130 gross.

This very typical buck is having fewer, but larger, points each year. It may be that he reached his potential for total bone growth early in life, and as the primary tines get longer, he is having to "rob Peter to pay Paul." This concept is frequently seen in antler development. At age 4½ he was a 6x7 typical before he broke some tines. At 5½ he barely tacked on that last point to be a 6x6 typical. At 6½ he's a tall-tined 5x6 typical. His spread is narrower than it used to be, but he's still a good-looking 150-class buck. He's not a particularly dominant animal. I wonder if social oppression may have affected his potential antler development.

*After **nine seasons** of watching and photographing this buck, he's as familiar as an old friend. Although there were two different years that I couldn't find him at all, he has been fairly visible most of the time, mainly because of his addiction to corn and other gastronomical delights. I don't think he misses many meals. If it's time to eat, he's there. He has a very recognizable face with interesting markings. His blocky body and lumbering gait are also easily known. During the season when he was 5½ and coming into his prime, he became quite aggressive. I've often wondered if the reason I couldn't find him at age 6½ might be tied in with the fact that he was at a prime breeding age, and he may have been traveling far and wide in the process. Antler-wise, he*

has been fairly consistent most of the years. The main exceptions were at age 4½ and again at 11½ when he grew an oddball drop tine close in on his right beam. It was in the same place both times. Most years he has wanted to be a 10-point typical. His G-4s have usually been uneven with the long and short sides alternating from year to year. Several years he barely even had the second G-4. At 5½ he had a beautifully symmetrical 10-point rack with fully developed G-4s. At 10½ he grew a large 4x4 typical rack. At 11½ he must have bumped his antlers in velvet, bending a beam and breaking a tine. I think he has aged remarkably well. At age 9½ or 10½, he easily could have been misjudged as 5½ or 6½ by someone who hadn't seen him before.

When it comes to gnarly, non-typical bucks, this has to be one of my all-time favorites. I had the honor of watching him on several occasions. Most times he was in the distance, but he was something to behold as he "worked" the meadows, chasing does and pushing other bucks around. By studying his appearance and behavior, as well as discussing previous years' sightings, I felt that he was 7½ years old the first year I saw him. His gross score was around 180. He declined a little when he was 8½. At 9½ the rancher told of seeing him in velvet with five tremendous brow points, but when I finally found him, three of them were broken from fighting. The next August he was seen on the ranch and was said to have had the biggest rack of his career, at 10½, with three major drop tines and five giant brow tines. He had 18 points total. I tried in vain to see him all that fall and the next, but I never laid an eye on him again. He was harvested at age 11½. He had double drop tines, a 25" inside spread, 15 points, and grossed 185.

This sequence is a good example of how environmental conditions can affect the antler development of a buck with good genetics. At 5½ years of age he was quite stout with a substantial 5x5 typical frame sporting a forked G-2 on the left. He had terrific brow tines. At age 6½, during an extreme drought year, he gained just a little tine length, but his mainframe reverted to a 4x5. His gross score may have declined slightly. It was hard to figure whether his antlers would improve or not. Then the rains came, and at 7½ he blossomed. He regained his 5x5 mainframe and much more. He grew a long common-base point, two hook-like stickers, and a couple of burr points. He was taken by a hunter that season, and his gross score was 181.

This buck lived in an area that was practically overrun by wild feral hogs. By the time he was 5½ and quite dominant among deer, he also became very belligerent with the feral hog population. This is very rare. Almost all whitetails, even large mature bucks, are extremely fearful of hogs. I've seen monster bucks flee in terror at the approach of small hogs, many times. But not this one. I've seen him stand his ground, time and time again, when hogs came into food plots and feeding areas. I dubbed him the "World's Bravest Whitetail." He commonly pushes the smaller hogs away, and he stands his ground with the big hogs. Even when he can't win, he always leaves with his dignity intact.

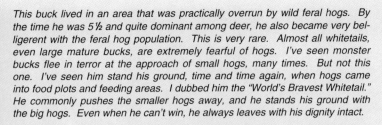

The "World's Bravest Whitetail" (see story above) is one of the most fearless and independent-minded whitetails I've ever seen. He's still alive and healthy at the ripe old age of 11. He's always been a very stout, muscular buck, and I think he was born with an attitude. He seems to go on about his business no matter who or what gets in his way. I've accidentally walked up on him way back in the brush on two or three occasions over the years, and each time he simply laid still and glared at me from 10 to 20 yards away. I got the impression that, had I not backed away and given him his space, he might well have come after me just like he does the hogs. He lives on a

hunted ranch but usually stays in several areas which receive light pressure. I couldn't find him at all during two of the eight years I've been tracking him, but he's been highly visible during the last few years. He's been on the "protected" list since he became so familiar. His antlers have been very consistent ever since he was 3½. He has always had 10 symmetrical points. He also had three sticker points when he was 7½, one at 8½, and a fork and two sticker points when he was 10½. His antler mass is modest compared to his body size and his attitude. Consequently, he usually breaks his antlers up badly during the rut. At 10½ he looks great and grosses in the mid-150s.

One year I was told of a very young buck that had seven or eight sticker points. I sat patiently in blinds for several days, but I didn't see him. Then, on the very last afternoon, he came prancing out of the woods. It was just my luck that he had already broken off one entire side of his antlers. Still, he was quite impressive for a 3½-year-old. He seemed "promising" to say the least. When I saw him the next season, he had improved, but he had already broken off three or four points by the time I found him. At 5½ he had a substantially heavier rack but had only two sticker points. He was killed in a buck fight and scored in the low 140s.

4½

5½

A narrow spread does not necessarily mean a poor set of antlers, and here's one example. This buck has been narrow during each of the three years that I've seen him.

At age 4½ he had about a 13-inch spread, a 5x5 typical frame, and two small sticker points. His gross score was in the mid-120s. At 5½ he had improved. His spread was about 14 inches, he had a 5x6 typical frame that was now much larger, and he had two large sticker points. He had become a 150-class buck.

At 6½ years of age he apparently damaged his right antler pedicel very early in the regeneration process. It caused him to grow a double beam and gave him a very narrow, lopsided set of antlers for the year. His inside spread was only about 10 or 11 inches, but he had six typical points on his left side and four points on each of the beams on his right side (14 points total). His gross score was well into the 150s.

An interesting thing happened during the season he was 6½. Hunters were on the lookout for this buck but had been unable to find him. I went out one day and found him, but something was different. I finally realized that he had broken off the smaller of the two double beams. It had changed his appearance. Many times bucks look very different late in the season after they've broken off substantial points.

6½

Field-aging wild bucks is always more difficult in the summertime. Most bucks that are anything less than fully mature tend to appear somewhat effeminate during this period, presenting small necks and soft-looking muscle tone. Studying their interactive behavior will help somewhat. This handsome buck added a fork and an extra point to his nine-point frame when he was 5½. At 7½ he grew a fully developed 5x5 typical frame with matched forks on both G-2s. Oddly enough, he lost both of his forks completely at age 8½.

Here's a buck that wanted to have lots of typical points. At 4½ he was a 6x7 typical. At 5½ he was a larger, 5x6 typical with a sticker point. I don't know what happened when he was 6½, but it must have been very traumatic. He may have been seriously injured the previous year, or maybe he just busted his pedicels severely. It lowered his social ranking substantially, even though he was very large and muscular. Bucks of all ages were dominant over him that year. At 8½ he grew a 150-class, 6x6 typical rack and regained his social status. I saw him at 9½, and he had a 9x6 all-typical frame grossing in the low 160s, but I couldn't get a photo.

This buck lived in an area of dense piney woods mixed with open meadows. He traveled long distances during the rut, sometimes moving several miles within a single day. At 5½ he was a typical 5x5 with a forked G-2 on his right. At 6½ he added another typical point on his left, becoming a 5x6. There were a couple of sticker points on his right side. Then, just to confuse me, his typical points switched sides at 7½, and his abnormal points disappeared altogether. At 7½ his gross score was in the high 150s.

The first time I ever saw this buck, I had sneaked way back into some heavy woods and was rattling antlers. He came raging in as though he were going to tear me up, and he was only a 3½-year-old. He had already broken some tines. The next season, when he was 4½, I saw him only once. For some reason his rack was spindly, and the G-4s were barely there. However, at 5½ he exploded. He was taken by a hunter that year and his inside spread was 26 inches. He had 12 points and was a 150-class buck.

117

3½

4½

5½

6½

I've been watching this old codger for eight seasons. His rack has never been monstrous, but his antlers have always been above average. At his best, his gross scores have been in the mid to upper 140s. There doesn't seem to be a non-typical bone in his body, except for the third little "unicorn" antler which he grew at age 9½. His markings are very attractive, and his face is easy to

recognize. He also has a nonchalant walking style that you can see a mile away. He's always been fairly dominant, but just in the last year or so, he seems to be getting more solitary and reclusive. Even so, any bucks which happen to invade his personal space are asking for trouble. He's still alive, and at 10½ his antlers have reverted to an eight-point frame with very heavy bases.

At age 4½ this buck was trying desperately to participate in breeding activities, but older, more experienced bucks were keeping him at bay. Notice that he had a small spot of pure white hair on his back. He was a very symmetrical 10-pointer. When he was 5½, he had a drop tine on the left, and the right beam was broken off. I wondered if there had been double drop tines, since he had been so symmetrical. At 6½ his left side was freakish but had no drop tine. He still had the spot of white hair. I never saw him again.

The first time I saw this buck he was already 5½ years old and very dominant. At 6½ he surprised me by sprouting three small drop tines near the ends of his beams. He also grew split brow tines. Before the year was over he had wounds and scars from head to tail. Maybe all that stress had something to do with his 7½-year-old rack. It was large but carried only seven points.

The first couple of years I observed this buck I saw him only in late summer. As time passed, I saw him more and more frequently. He was a big-bodied, dominant buck at age 6½. Though his mainframe was smaller, his antlers were more interesting at 5½ when he had 13 points. He is one of the less graceful whitetail bucks that I've known, walking and running with an uneven, stumbling gait.

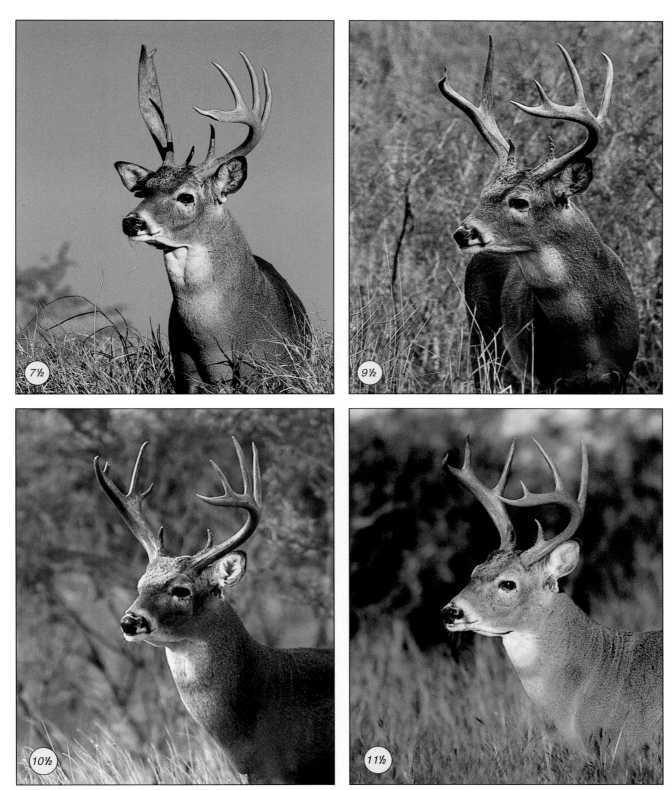

At 7½ years of age, this buck had suffered severe damage to his right antler pedicel. The antler was very freakish. With less severe injuries, an antler usually comes back to its normal configuration the next year. However, with a profound injury, the antler-growing mechanism sometimes "remembers" the injury-caused configuration and tries to repeat it. This buck had been a purely typical buck previous to his injury. It's interesting to note that as each year went by, his right antler came a little closer to being normal, as though the "memory" were fading. His social status was initially diminished, but at 11½ he has regained some of his social standing.

The first time I saw this buck, I knew he was something special. He was only 2½ years old and had 12 heavy points. He made impressive gains at age 3½ and even more impressive gains at 4½. He remained large at 5½ but lost some of his extra points and character, becoming more symmetrical overall. At age 4½ his gross score was in the mid to high 160s, maybe more.

It seems that this buck's genetic programming never intended that he would have world-class antlers. However, it's hard to be sure. The area where he lived was overpopulated well beyond its carrying capacity. Had he been on a better nutritional plane, he might have surprised us. He lived for three more years, but I wasn't able to get good photos. His antlers declined to a small 4x5 frame at age 9½, but he came back with a respectable 5x6 typical rack when he was 10½. At 11½ he was taken down by a pack of coyotes.

Maybe I'm just a sucker for wide, laid-out, multi-pointed antlers, but I think this is a beautiful buck. He had nice colors and markings, and he had some very interesting antler characteristics. He grew one to three forked tines each year. At 4½ his right G-3 was forked. At 5½ both his right G-3 and his left G-2 were forked. Then at 6½ both G-3s were forked and both brow tines split. The year he was 6½, he had 16 points total, although four of them were small. At 7½ he gained mass and had a very symmetrical 5x5

typical frame with deep forks in both G-3s. When he was 8½ his left brow tine was split, and he had forks on his right G-2 and both G-3s. His gross score was in the 160s during each of his last three years. This buck was highly aggressive. He invariably had his antlers all broken up from fighting by the time the rut was under way. He became quite secretive as he got older, and I didn't see him much after he was 5½. I found him only once when he was 6½ and once when he was 7½, and I barely got the two photos above.

127

5½

6½

7½

If you like classic, typical bucks, then this is your man. He was a big 6x6 typical when he was 5½, 6½ and 7½. At 7½ he had a small sticker point. His antlers were perhaps the most impressive when he was 6½, grossing in the 160s. This buck had a very haughty personality, strutting around as though he owned the place. And maybe he did! During his prime years he was unquestionably

the "king of the hill." He was very dominant, always threatening other bucks. He was a frequent fighter, and I saw him twice with substantial injuries. When he reached the age of 8½, his antlers actually improved from the previous year. He was a 7x7 typical, though one small point is broken off in the photo. The first time I ever saw another buck intimidate him was when he was 9½. Then he disappeared.

This is the quintessential eight-pointer. He is the epitome of "average" where whitetail antlers are concerned. It's remarkable how consistent he has been for seven seasons. If the years weren't marked on the photos, it would be almost impossible to put them in the correct sequence. The fact that he's in velvet in each of these shots makes it even more difficult to age him, particularly

since he ages so gracefully. These photos show him in velvet because I've rarely seen him in hard antlers — only a few times over the seven years that I've watched him. Some bucks can be easily located during the summer but then be very difficult to find later in the season. Others are just the opposite. This buck is rather handsome, but on average his gross score is only in the mid-120s.

The genetic blueprint for this buck's antlers must be quite inflexible. There has been very little variability in his antler traits from year to year. He has always been an eight-pointer except for age 4½ when he had nine points. His short brow tines consistently lay inward and backward. His right G-3 is always shorter and more horizontal than his left G-3. And above all else, those

incredibly long beams are forever wrapping around horizontally, as though trying to touch. I measured his right-hand shed antler from age 6½ and found the beam to be 26 inches long. The forward-curving G-2 was almost 11 inches. His beams lay back before they sweep around and turn inward. At age 7½ he was almost exactly the same size as at age 6½. He is a 140-class buck.

When I first saw him at age 4½, I had great, high hopes for this buck. He had a 7x7 purely typical frame and by all appearances had room to grow. His mass was good for his age, and tine length was average or better. He was very standoffish and easily intimidated by older and more dominant bucks. The next season I found him in the same area, but his antlers had changed somewhat. He was now a 5x7 with common-base points on one side. The size of his frame was about the same. He was not at all dominant for a 5½-year-old. I didn't see him at all when he was 6½. In fact, I wondered if he was still alive. The following season I was on the ranch

8½

9½

working a completely different area and guess what? Up popped a nice 10-pointer, and there he was. It was unquestionably the same buck, but his antler mainframe had become a 5x5 typical frame, still in the same shape as his old 7x7 frame. At 8½ I saw him ranging widely throughout the ranch. His antlers had gone back to 5x7 but in a slightly different configuration than before. Late that season he was apparently "hooked" in the testicles by another buck. He appeared to be injured quite severely, but his body some- how repaired itself. I thought it might cause his antlers to grow abnormally, but it didn't. At 9½ he grew a nice 5x5 typical rack.

This sequence illustrates the unhappy life of a bizarre little buck which I observed for several years. I saw this buck a number of times during late summer periods as I watched bachelor groups on a ranch. He was very "puny" to begin with, and he took a beating from virtually all the other bucks on a regular basis. I don't know if he was genetically inferior, if he had some illness or disease, or if he just got off to a bad start, and the incredible social pressure stifled his development. He was kicked and pushed around unmercifully. It's hard to believe that in the bottom photo the "puny" buck is 6½ years old, and the buck kicking him is 5½.

This buck certainly fooled me. At age 3½ and again at 4½ he was a mediocre eight-pointer showing no indication that he would ever be anything more. There were no signs of any G-4s. Then when he was 5½, I could hardly believe it was the same deer. He had become a well-developed 5x5 with large stickers on both G-2s. His gross score went from the low 120s to the 150s.

I still have high hopes for this buck. At age 3½ he looked fairly promising with large brow tines and a respectable 5x5 typical frame. At 4½ he has made some substantial gains. Though they are uneven, his brow tines are very big, the larger one being eight or nine inches long. He now carries a 5x6 typical frame with exceptionally long, high beams. He's a solid 150-class buck.

Each buck is unique in his own way, but this one is more unusual than most. Can you see how he is so different from most other bucks? He has absolutely NO TAIL whatsoever, not even a stub. At age 4½ he had a nice 4x5 typical frame, but it wasn't very massive. The next season, at 5½, he had moved his territory almost a mile, but he was still easy to recognize. He developed a larger, heavier, 5x5 mainframe. The G-2s and G-3s now have some bumps and ridges on them. If he lives another year or two, I suspect there will be sticker points. Once, I was watching him closely while he was staring into the distance as whitetails do when assessing possible dangers. At the point when he decided that everything was OK, when most deer flick their tails and move on, the bump at the end of his backbone jumped back and forth just before he took his first step. He had instinctively wagged the tail he didn't have.

I first saw this buck when he was 3½ years old. He had a 4x4 typical frame with one small "blip" of a sticker point. He was a small-bodied deer and was afraid of most other bucks. The next season I saw him once, but only at a distance, and he was about the same. However, another year passed, and at 5½ he has grown to be a substantial 150-class buck with long tines and big sticker points. He's no longer timid around other bucks. I'm anxious to see what he will do the next time around.

As a middle-aged buck, and even at maturity, this buck was nice but average. It wasn't until he was fully into the "old" category, at 7½ years of age, that he really blossomed. His antlers changed from his lifelong 4x4 frame to a very tall-tined 5x5 frame. It's a little difficult to see him as a 7½-year-old with that tiny summer neck, but he is. I rarely saw this buck after he removed his velvet.

When he was middle-aged, this tall-tined buck was very curious and pushy, always getting too close and sparring with other, more dominant bucks. They would push him away repeatedly, but he would keep coming back, over and over again. He was very dominant at maturity. It was a little surprising when he changed from his eight-point mainframe to a solid ten-point frame at age 7½. When he did, his extremely long G-2s were shortened, and his sticker disappeared, as though that amount of bone had to be traded in to get the new G-4s. Unfortunately, he was killed by another buck during that season. His gross score was measured at 153.

After seeing this buck at 2½, 3½ and 4½, I was anxiously hoping to see him turn into something gigantic. However, he apparently was one of those rare individuals which grow into their potential at a very young age and never get any better. He was a 5x5 at 2½, a 6x6 at 3½, and a 6x7 at 4½. He was a 6x6 thereafter with about the same size frame. At his best he was a 140-class buck.

I saw this buck repeatedly from one of my fencerow blinds. This particular ranch is hunted quite thoroughly, and frankly, I never expected to see him again after watching him in the early fall when he was 6½. I was photographing in one small area that was usually not pressured too much, and apparently he was smart enough to know that. I was amazed to see him reach the age of 10½.

10½

11½

The very first time I ever saw this buck, he was quite old. The rancher had already told me about him, as he was seen very frequently. I saw him many times in widely scattered parts of the rather large property. He was very dominant and still heavily involved in the breeding rituals, and he traveled far and wide in the process. I even rattled him up a couple of times when I was way back in the brush. This old buck was just dripping with character and attitude. I never saw him back down from any standoff or fight. In fact, early one foggy morning (before there was enough light for photography), I watched him have a knock-down, drag-out struggle with another mature buck. He

flipped the other buck onto his back at least twice. He was absolutely fearless. When I first observed him, his antlers were already in some decline from the time when he had been in his prime. The rancher told me that in years past he had grown as many as 14 points and a larger mainframe. When you see a buck for the first time at a truly advanced age, it's impossible to determine exactly how old he is. During my first year on the ranch, the owner thought this buck was well over 10 years old. Clearly, he was well into the "old" category. I saw him for five years in a row before he died of natural causes. For the sake of our examples, we will start him at 10½, knowing that it's just an educated guess. When he was 11½ he was still fighting frequently, and he injured a foot in one such scuffle. He could hardly walk, and I think that the injury may have contributed to the sharp decline in his antler quality the following year. Though he had smaller antlers when he was 12½, he was still a "fighting machine." During one of his fights, he tore his lip and injured the top of his head, ripping loose a piece of scalp. The next year, at 13½, he grew extra burr points, some growing down the back of his head. Altogether he had 19 measurable points. At 14½ both body and antlers went into serious decline and he passed away. Considering his longevity, as well as his dominance, he may have significantly influenced the gene pool on that property.

4½

5½

6½

7½

I observed this buck for nine seasons. His sequence emphatically illustrates an occurrence which is commonly seen in the whitetail world. His genetic programming only allowed for an eight-point mainframe, no matter how well he was fed (nutrition was plentiful) or no matter how mature he became (he became very old). He had a huge, muscular body, and he was a handsome

buck with beautiful markings and the rather rare, amber-colored eyes that a few deer have. He was the type of big eight-pointer that tends to become very dominant over other prime, better-antlered bucks. The heavy body, bad attitude and long, high tines gave him a distinct fighting advantage for most of his life. He was still perfectly healthy at age 12½, but he was killed in a fight with another buck.

2½

3½

4½

This buck is a perfect example of just how unimportant scoring can be when it comes to pure whitetail appreciation. Almost everybody likes wide-racked bucks, and this one had an inside spread of 24 to 26 inches for four years in a row. Yet, whether he had eight, nine or ten points, he was still only a 140-class buck at his best. Even so, I know very few people who could look at him at age 5½ and not be a little impressed regardless of score. He's the kind of buck that most of us would look at and say, "Who cares?" On the other hand, for someone who IS extremely interested in score, this is the type of buck that can be a grand disappointment. A quick glance alone could easily mislead a person into thinking his score might be much higher than it is.

This buck made a remarkable gain in spread at the age of 3½. When I first saw him as a super wide buck, I didn't realize that I already knew him. Then I finally recognized his face from the previous year. The markings were unmistakable. Oddly, he had one or two acorn points in three of the five years that I saw him. I don't know if he was just clumsy and tended to bump his velvet antlers a lot, or if the extremely wide spread caused him to bump himself more frequently. Also, I thought it was highly unusual that the shape of his antler mainframe changed when he was 6½. At first glance the rack at 6½ seems smaller than the year before, but the main difference is in the shape of the beams. They reverted back to the same shape that they had when he was 2½ years old.

I saw this buck a total of only four or five times over the four-season time span covered here. He seems to be a particularly cautious and fearful deer and is subordinate to most other bucks of the same age. He has a gray forehead and very little white around his eyes. Though all of his antler characteristics are fairly ordinary in scope, he is still a handsome 140-class buck.

When I first saw the thin-bodied deer standing in the road ahead, something was obviously awry. His rump was much too white. As you can see, it turned out that he had no tail other than a small tuft of hair. He was easy to recognize after that. By the time he was 6½, he had 11 points, but he grossed only in the high 120s. I saw him all over the ranch that year, then never saw him again.

In his earlier years, I saw this buck mostly during late summer. At age 4½ I didn't see him at all, but when he was 5½, it seemed that he was everywhere I went. Although he was of average stature, he was quite dominant at 5½. He didn't have remarkable colorations or markings, but he did have a very distinctive, recognizable gait. At 5½ his gross score was in the low to mid-130s.

This rather strangely antlered buck was already so old when I first saw him that I couldn't be sure about his age, but I felt that 8½ was a good estimate. He was fearful of most prime-aged bucks. The weird drop tine may have been a one-year anomaly, since it disappeared the following year. Now that he's reached the age of 10½, his antlers have come back to a more normal configuration.

This buck had a very stocky build at age 4½, but he didn't really have the antlers to match it. This type of antler mainframe with wide open beams will sometimes develop into a super wide spread. However, it didn't happen in this case. At 7½ he had developed a 5x5 frame with some common-base points. When he was 8½ his antlers became very weird, uneven and gnarly.

Here's a story I've seen repeated over and over again — another "fighter," a buck with a really bad, dominant attitude. The photo at age 3½ was taken during the peak of the rut. He had ripped one antler completely out of its pedicel. At age 5½ he broke off his left beam while fighting. About a month after I photographed him at age 6½, he was found dead, gored by another buck during a fight.

This buck has a highly recognizable double throat patch. It seems that he puts so much energy into growing brow tines that there's not much left for the remainder of the rack. Other than G-1s, his tines have been extremely weak each year. Curiously, his brow tines were deeply forked at 8½, but at 9½ the forks had moved. He then had single brow tines and stickers on each G-2. He has remained active into old age. Last fall, when he was 9½, I watched him mount a doe during a cold, rainy December afternoon.

I rattled up this particular buck several times over the years. He was active and quite dominant, but somehow he managed to take pretty good care of himself. It must have been due to skill or ability, because he wasn't especially massive in either antlers or body. Strangely, his ninth point moved around on his rack every year, from his left G-2 to his right beam, then to his right G-2.

I've seen this buck many times over the years, but rarely when he was standing still. It seems that the only time he stands still is when he's peering from behind a fortress of thick brush. He's not a very dominant deer. I suppose that makes him all the more jumpy, since he's just about as fearful of other bucks as he is of humans. Apparently his antler blueprint calls for the old basic eight-

point mainframe, because that's what he's grown every year. In his case, the repeating mechanism also includes some modest sticker points. His antlers are showing one trend that is unusual. As he is getting older, his spread is getting wider. In most cases when bucks get very old, the spread becomes more narrow. At his best, at age 7½, his gross score was in the mid to upper 130s.

After finding this buck for seven out of eight seasons, he is another "old friend." In terms of antlers, he never showed a great deal of promise. He's been a nine-pointer most of the time, though he made it all the way to 10 points a couple of years. His right side is generally stronger than his left, and his brow tines usually point inward. By the time he was 6½, he looked pretty

good. I missed seeing him at age 7½. When he was 8½ years old he grew a 6x4 rack. The year he was 9½ was a terrible drought year, and that may have contributed to his small eight-point frame. However, the rains came with the next year, and he improved to a respectable, symmetrical 5x5 mainframe at age 10½. The odd shape of his body hints at his elderly status.

It's easy to see that whitetail faces are as individual as the faces of people once you get your eyes pried away from the antlers for a moment. This middle-aged buck has an attractive face, but he doesn't have any remarkable features. Nevertheless, if you got a good look at him and zeroed in on his face, as in this photo, there's a good chance you would remember him if you saw him again.

I've only seen this buck twice. The sightings were about a year apart in time and about a mile apart in distance. With only two brief encounters, notice how easy it is to see that it is the same buck in both photos. The shape of his body, the shape of his antler mainframe, and the way that he carries himself are all recognizable by themselves. In combination, the recognition is unmistakable.

Velvet antlers don't get a lot better than this, especially on 4½-year-old bucks. He may look a bit dainty with his big eyes and small summer neck, but that's about to change. It's almost time to remove the velvet. Soon the hormones will begin raging, his muscle tone will change, and his appearance will be very different. He's a spectacular 180-class buck, maybe even 190-class.

Whitetails frequently display a "stomping" behavior when they are suspicious or fearful. That's exactly what the buck at the upper left is doing. He thinks he may have seen or heard something dangerous. There are also other reasons for whitetails to stomp. The buck at the upper right has just been whipped in a brief scuffle with another buck, and in the process he apparently hurt his leg. He stretched it out and stomped it over and over as though he were trying to get rid of a cramp. The buck at the bottom is stomping for yet another reason. He's standing with a young doe that's coming into estrus, and she is laying down and ignoring him. He walked up to her and stomped the ground repeatedly, staring at her all the while as though to demand that she get up.

Whitetails are extremely agile, and they use their agility in many ways. They twist and turn like contortionists, constantly checking out all directions for possible sources of danger. They can turn their heads in virtually any direction without moving their feet at all. The buck at the bottom is wildly wrenching his neck back and forth, trying to dislodge an intruder from his ear.

Bucks occasionally pick up a little excess baggage as they go about their daily business. The buck on the left was showing off earlier by thrashing some bushes to intimidate other bucks in the vicinity. I didn't see him, but I could hear all the noise he was making. A small broken limb lodged in his antlers. It's quite common to see bucks walking around with pieces of vegetation stuck in their antlers during the pre-rut period as well as during the rut. The buck on the right has been rooting around in the leaves, looking for acorns.

This buck has developed huge tumors which are growing on his belly. The previous year he was a large, typical 10-pointer. Serious illness or disease frequently causes antlers to change from their usual configuration. In this case the buck grew a double beam, a double brow tine and a forked tine. Other deer always notice when a buck becomes sick or disfigured, and they usually shun him.

Whitetails are subject to many dangers. The buck at the top has apparently been bitten by a rattlesnake. I can't prove that, but it seems most likely. He had been observed only two days before and was perfectly normal then. There is a large population of rattlesnakes in the area. The swelling went down, and he survived. The buck at the bottom wasn't so lucky. Just the day before, he had been walking around normally. Chances are he was killed while fighting another buck. Then coyotes or hogs, or both, did the rest.

Dominance is a big issue to whitetails all year long. During the summer, when their antlers are soft, they fight with their hooves. They're not at all bashful about expressing themselves, and they can be quite vicious. Frequently, the more dominant buck will just push the other buck at first. Then, if the other buck doesn't leave or show submission, the more dominant deer will let him have it.

The antlers of these two exceptional bucks are constructed differently, but they both score about the same. What one buck lacks in mass is made up with tine length, and vice versa. We know that the gross score for each is approximately 198 because both deer were later found dead of natural causes, and the antlers were measured. The buck at the top wasn't found for almost a year.

Every big buck was once a tiny fawn. The transformations that a fawn goes through on his way to maturity are quite incredible. When comparing the fawn at the top with the mature buck at the bottom, it is apparent that everything doesn't change. The grace and beauty are constant all along the way. I found this long-beamed buck out in an open area where he was chasing a doe.

This very alert buck is still soaking wet from the light rain that's been falling for the past hour. He's a great-looking, 150-class buck just coming into his prime at age 5½. He did a lot of posturing, scraping and lip-curling as I watched, but I'm not sure whether or not he has what it takes to be a dominant buck. When posturing with other bucks, he backed down almost as often as he prevailed.

Summertime is a time of gentle beauty in the land of the whitetail. The youngsters at the top of the page are big pals now, but just give them two or three more years and see what happens in the fall of the year. They won't be buddies any more as they vie for dominance and breeding rights. The living has apparently been easy for the buck at the bottom. He's as fat as a pig.

The scene at the top of the page is almost too pretty to be real. The hot weather of summer turns waterholes into deer magnets, both for the drinking water and the lush vegetation found in such places. I took the photo at the bottom from my truck. As I quietly came around a curve in a dirt road, I caught these three bucks out in the middle of an open meadow. They didn't stay there for long.

The buck on the left is very impressive with plenty of points and lots of mass. He's watching a doe. The time is September, and he's just beginning to see his female meadow-mates in a different light. The buck at the upper right is performing a lip curl with great intensity. He seems to be enjoying it immensely. The buck at the bottom right is checking out the branches over a scrape.

During the rut, bucks sometimes travel very long distances in search of does. Two to five miles is commonplace, and fifteen to twenty miles is not out of the question. Bucks that have been following a relatively predictable routine may suddenly disappear for days or even weeks at a time. Some bucks get so side-tracked that they don't make it back to home base until after the season.

During the summer and early fall, the order of the day is to eat and then eat some more. A buck needs to build up his fat reserves as much as possible to ready himself for the very demanding times of the rut when he may go for long periods of time with very little food. This buck is eating a "maypop," the fruit of the passion vine which grows in the southeastern U.S.

It works for me. This is an extremely unusual buck with a super wide spread and quadruple drop tines. He's been observed for quite a number of years and each year he has grown either double, triple or quadruple drop tines. Of the relatively few bucks which grow drop tines, many are inconsistent, producing these anomalies on a sporadic basis or, in many cases, only once and never again.

Drop tines seem to be everybody's favorite points. They're highly unpredictable, they come in all manner of shapes and sizes, and only a small percentage of bucks ever grow them. Both bucks at the top have double drop tines, and each buck at the bottom has a single, very long drop tine. Both of the bucks at the bottom were seen the previous year ... with no drop tines at all.

The two bucks in the top photo have been sparring in a foggy field, and now they've been distracted by a minor disturbance, the approach of another deer. Unlike serious fights, sparring matches are easily interrupted. The buck at the bottom is working the edge of a brushline in the early morning light. He's not necessarily looking for a fight, but he's probably fully prepared for one.

The wide-antlered buck at the top popped out of nowhere at just about noon on a windy October day. He has a most unusual face. The bucks at the bottom are hard into a serious battle. Whitetail bucks really do fight a lot. Mortality from fighting may be considerably higher than what is generally thought. Each year I learn of many bucks that have been killed by other bucks.

Try though we may, the vast majority of our whitetail sightings will be fleeting moments. And it seems that the bigger the buck, the more fleeting the moment. Each of the shots on this page was grabbed from a very short window of opportunity. Since they're now captured on film where we can study them at leisure, it's easy to imagine that these moments lasted much longer than they really did.

Whitetails are extremely good at "getting away." Whenever danger presents itself, their reaction is instantaneous. Their escape plans are mostly foolproof, and the mechanism that sets the plans into action has a hair trigger. Most of us are far more familiar with the backside view of a whitetail buck than with the frontal perspective, and that's not likely to change. It's part of our lot in life.

If this rare glimpse is the kind of sight that you enjoy, there are four things you need — good wildlife managers to create conditions for such sights to be possible, physical access to these places, a working knowledge of the lifestyles and behaviors of white-tailed deer, and lots of plain ol' good luck. I'm not sure which of the four is the hardest to come by, but I suspect it's the luck.

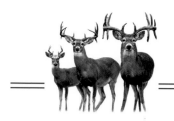 # THE WHITETAIL FRONTIER

This scene fairly well epitomizes the mystique which draws us in and holds us tight. I had seen this buck briefly the previous week, but he had been too far away and moving too fast for me to see very much. I had just about given up on seeing him again. Then, just before dusk, as the afterglow of sundown hit the sky, he was suddenly there. He's a beautiful, long-beamed, 160-class buck.

Those of us who really love whitetails have been all over the whitetail map during the last 20 to 30 years. And now we're picking up the pace. There are countless individuals hard at work blazing new trails through the complicated maze of facts, myths, possibilities, and definite maybes. Our enthusiasm about the lives and lifestyles of deer is as boundless as whitetail truths are elusive.

Great progress has been made. There's no doubt about that. This is due in no small part to the small army of researchers and biologists who have devoted their careers to searching out the facts about deer, and who have helped to educate us on the ways and the wiles of the whitetail. Also, much of the credit for the current state of affairs goes to the countless ranchers and landowners who have spent their own time and resources learning about deer and experimenting with the different whitetail management practices which have evolved. As with any learning process, nothing works like trial and error when it

Whitetail managers are working toward a time when they can produce more bucks like the non-typical above or the 190-class monster on the left. Some people think that it's just around the corner, but others believe it will never happen. For that matter, many people aren't so sure that it would be a good thing for "super bucks" to become commonplace. It might destroy some of the mystery which we enjoy so much.

comes to discovering the truth about things. With whitetails, there's never a shortage of "error."

Today's average whitetail enthusiasts, most of whom are hunters, know so much more about deer than they did just 10 years ago that there's no comparison. As always, there are still plenty of people in search of the so-called "magic bullet," looking for an easy way or a shortcut to help them find big bucks. However, more and more people have come to realize that education is the key — education and a little common sense.

Even with all the current information available, there are still some people who seem to have been unaffected by the

*Even though it may be unlikely that "super bucks" will ever become commonplace, scenes like this one seem to be more frequent than they were a few years ago. These **are** the "good ol' days." I came upon this buck as I was easing through the woods during a light rain. It was cold and miserable, but I knew the peak of the rut was near. It's hard to find big deer when you stay in camp where it's warm and comfortable. At the time of this photo he had obviously seen me, but he also had another, more powerful distraction. He was standing with a doe that was in estrus, and for whatever reason, she didn't seem to be afraid of me. He wanted to run, but the urge to breed was overpowering. A few minutes later he mounted and bred her as I watched, and then they ran away. That night I proudly related the story to the ranch owner. He just chuckled and said, "Yep, we'll probably harvest that doe during doe season."*

explosion of new data which has otherwise transformed the entire thinking about whitetails. I'm amazed when I still occasionally hear folks boasting that their ranch or hunting club "manages" deer by taking only those bucks which are "eight points or better." A lot of good country has been "top-ended" by such practices over the years. It doesn't take too many years of systematic removal of the best genetics from a herd for overall antler quality to deteriorate. Then, if and when

people realize the error, it can take many years to get back to where they started. It seems that one of the biggest problems in dealing with whitetails is that it's so easy to mess things up, yet so difficult to fix them.

At any rate, the majority of today's whitetail nuts are on a more positive track, and they're getting more educated all the time. There's tremendous interest in whitetail publications, research, seminars, hunting shows, and all manner of related functions and products.

For future generations to have the opportunity to feel the emotion that comes with a sighting like this, it's our responsibility to see that whitetail education continues to be dispersed. For instance, many people still don't understand that excessive "conservation" and "protection" can cause whitetail populations to boom and bust. Management is the key. And knowledge is the prerequisite.

If you're a whitetail nut, the sighting of a buck like this might cause your internal hard drive to crash. Giant antlers can cause every synapse in your body to overload, effectively wrecking your nervous system. I suppose you could get this type of "rush" in other ways, but chasing whitetails is much safer than bungee jumping or sky diving and much more pleasant than a shark attack.

Scientifically, the next steps are primarily in the area of genetic research. Controlled breeding programs have been in place for many years, and their numbers are increasing at a rapid pace. Part of today's cutting edge is focused on the identification of the specific genes which are responsible for antler growth and characteristics. Practices such as artificial insemination are being utilized more and more to help speed up the results of breeding programs.

Who knows what the future will bring? It will definitely include more intensive management of whitetails than ever before. Whitetail sperm banks are already in existence. Specialty helicopter crews now use "net guns" to capture and relocate scores of wild deer in just a few hours time. Deer from different regions and different bloodlines are being cross-bred much like cattle. Whitetail diseases are being treated and/or eradicated. Nutritional needs are being micro-managed and studied in every detail.

Will technology eventually create such an artificiality that it could destroy the mystique which brought us here in the first place? In extreme cases that might be possible. Certainly we don't want to see whitetails come to share the same status as livestock. Nobody wants to hunt a Hereford.

For most of us, the real final frontier of whitetail enlightenment lies in the accurate perception of their lives and times — the true understanding of how whitetails live, develop, behave and age under **natural** circumstances. We want the knowledge. We need the mystery.

Whitetails are amazing creatures, and their future is largely in our hands. It's an enormous responsibility, but the rewards are well worth the effort. When this buck appeared, the sun had been down for a long time, and it was getting so dark that I had abandoned the camera just to watch a few deer on the hillside. One moment he wasn't there, and in the next moment he was. Out of nothing more than a bare hilltop and a long gone sundown, he had created the kind of scene that is the stuff of whitetail dreams.